Effective Instruction
for English Language Learners

TEACHING PRACTICES THAT WORK

Diane Lapp and Douglas Fisher, Series Editors

Designed specifically for busy teachers who value evidence-based instructional practices, books in this series offer ready-to-implement strategies and tools to promote student engagement, improve teaching and learning across the curriculum, and support the academic growth of all students in our increasingly diverse schools. Written by expert authors with extensive experience in "real-time" classrooms, each concise and accessible volume provides useful explanations and examples to guide instruction, as well as step-by-step methods and reproducible materials, all in a convenient large-size format for ease of photocopying.

35 Strategies for Guiding Readers through Informational Texts
Barbara Moss and Virginia S. Loh

The Effective Teacher's Guide, Second Edition:
50 Ways to Engage Students and Promote Interactive Learning
Nancy Frey

Dare to Differentiate, Third Edition: Vocabulary Strategies for All Students
Danny Brassell

Effective Instruction for English Language Learners:
Supporting Text-Based Comprehension and Communication Skills
Julie Jacobson, Kelly Johnson, and Diane Lapp

Effective Instruction for English Language Learners

Supporting Text-Based Comprehension and Communication Skills

Julie Jacobson
Kelly Johnson
Diane Lapp

Series Editors' Note
by Diane Lapp and Douglas Fisher

THE GUILFORD PRESS
New York   London

© 2011 The Guilford Press
A Division of Guilford Publications, Inc.
72 Spring Street, New York, NY 10012
www.guilford.com

Printed in the United States of America

This book is printed on acid-free paper.

Last digit is print number: 9 8 7 6 5 4 3 2 1

Library of Congress Cataloging-in-Publication Data

Jacobson, Julie.
  Effective instruction for English language learners : supporting text-based
comprehension and communication skills / by Julie Jacobson, Kelly Johnson,
and Diane Lapp.
    p. cm. — (Teaching Practices That Work)
  Includes bibliographical references and index.
  ISBN 978-1-60918-252-6 (pbk.: alk. paper)
  1. English language—Study and teaching—Foreign speakers.   2. Content area
reading.   3. Education, Bilingual.   I. Johnson, Kelly, 1971–   II. Lapp, Diane.
III. Title.
  PE1128.A2J34 2011
  372.652′1—dc22
                                                        2011007158

About the Authors

Julie Jacobson, PhD, is an English language and Spanish teacher at Scripps Ranch High School in San Diego and a faculty member in the Department of Teacher Education at San Diego State University. Dr. Jacobson has published articles in many journals, including *The California Reader* and the *Journal of Adolescent and Adult Literacy*. Her focus is on supporting the language development of students who are acquiring English as an additional language.

Kelly Johnson, PhD, is a faculty member in teacher education at San Diego State University and a classroom teacher at Health Sciences High and Middle College in San Diego. She has taught grades from kindergarten to college and has appeared in many instructional videos on teacher modeling, assessment and instruction, effective grouping, and writing instruction. A recipient of the California Reading Association's Constance McCullough Research Award for her dissertation on the topic of assessment and diagnostic instruction, Dr. Johnson (formerly Dr. Kelly Moore) has published articles in many journals, including *The Reading Teacher*, *The California Reader*, *The Reading Professor*, and *Literacy*. She is coauthor of the books *Designing Responsive Curriculum: Planning Lessons That Work* and *Teaching Literacy in First Grade*. Her focus is on assessment and small-group guided instructional practice.

Diane Lapp, EdD, is Distinguished Professor of Education in the Department of Teacher Education at San Diego State University. She has taught elementary and middle school and currently works as an 11th- and 12th-grade English teacher at Health Sciences High and Middle College in San Diego. Her research and instruction focus on issues related to struggling readers and writers who live in economically deprived urban settings, and their families and teachers. Dr. Lapp has published numerous journal articles, columns, chapters, books, and children's materials. She has received the Outstanding Teacher Educator of the Year Award from the International Reading Association (IRA), among other honors, and is a member of both the IRA and the California Reading Hall of Fame.

Series Editors' Note

A s our schools continue to grow in linguistic, cultural, and socioeconomic diversity, educators are committed to implementing instruction that supports both individual and collective growth within their classrooms. In tandem with teacher commitment, schools recognize the need to support teacher collaboration on issues related to implementing, evaluating, and expanding instruction to ensure that all students will graduate from high school with the skills needed to succeed in the workforce. Through our work with teachers across the country, we've become aware of the need for books that can be used to support professional collaboration by grade level and subject area. With these teachers' questions in mind, we decided that a series of books was needed that modeled "real-time" teaching and learning within classroom instruction. Thus the series *Teaching Practices That Work* was born.

Books in this series are distinguished by offering instructional examples that have been studied and refined within authentic classroom settings. Each book is written by one or more educators who are well connected to everyday classroom instruction. Because the series editors are themselves classroom teachers as well as professors, each instructional suggestion has been closely scrutinized for its validity.

Designing rigorous instruction that supports and scaffolds literacy learning with content learning for English language learners (ELLs) often seems like a daunting task, especially when students have varying levels of English language and literacy proficiency. Since instruction must accommodate this wide range of strengths and needs, the dilemma becomes how to design, implement, and manage teaching that is appropriate for individuals, small groups, and whole groups. The authors of *Effective Instruction for English Language Learners: Supporting Text-Based Comprehension and Communication Skills* have addressed these concerns through lessons designed to develop students' skills with pronunciation, grammar, vocabulary, and fluency as supports for comprehension. Each lesson focuses on developing one of these skills for either beginning, intermediate, or advanced learners and also includes extensions of the same lesson for the other two groups of students. For example, if the core lesson addresses intermediate language learners, extensions are given for the beginning and advanced learners.

To help with the implementation of these scaffolded lessons, the authors frame each one through the lens of a gradual release-of-instruction model. The lessons begin with a clear statement of the purpose, research base, and content—including relevant Common Core and TESOL standards—and are followed by ideas for teacher modeling, guided practice, and projects for peer collaboration and independent work. Book selections identified by English proficiency level accompany each lesson, as do ideas for integrating new web-based literacies. Taken together, the features of each lesson support instruction in regular classrooms where teachers are working to provide ELLs with access to mainstream curriculum while developing their academic English.

We invite you into the "real-time" teaching offered in this book and hope you'll find this series useful as you validate and expand your teaching repertoire. And if you have an idea for a book, please contact us!

DIANE LAPP
DOUGLAS FISHER

Contents

Appendix

Introduction

How Does This Book Address the Needs of English Language Learners?

This book has been designed to provide teachers with research-supported instructional practices that foster language, literacy, and content-area growth for all students whose performance indicates that they have beginning, intermediate, or advanced levels of language proficiency. Instruction of this type is greatly needed inasmuch as the school-age population of English language learners (ELLs) continues to grow. In 1990 1 in 20 schoolchildren were ELLs. In 2005 the number had increased to one in nine, and current projections suggest that ELLs now "make up approximately 25% of the total student population" (Freeman & Crawford, 2008, p. 12). Within the next 20 years, projections suggest that one in every four school-age students may be an ELL (Capps et al., 2005; Garcia & Montavon, 2007; National Clearinghouse for Language Acquisition, 2008). Though the concentration varies across different regions, the number of students in the United States whose home language is not English was more than 10 million in 2008 (National Center for Education Statistics, 2010). Much of the current growth among English learners has occurred in states and school districts that previously enrolled only small numbers of students whose first language was not English. Although the languages spoken are quite diverse, with ELLs speaking more than 400 languages, 80% speak Spanish and are from a Mexican heritage (Kindler, 2002).

Current trends toward mandated assessments call for annual state assessments of all ELLs. For example: "The Common Core State Standards for English Language Arts (ELA) articulate rigorous grade-level expectations in the areas of speaking, listening, reading, and writing to prepare all students to be college and career ready, including English language learners" (Common Core State Standards Initiative, 2010).

The Need for Curriculum That Supports Self-Efficacy

As the ELL student population has increased, so too has the need for the development of special language-learning instructional approaches to promote each student's sense of worth (Echevarría, Vogt, & Short, 2007; Ovando, Collier, & Combs, 2003). The development of self-efficacy in academic settings is often difficult for English learners because they must concurrently deal with multiple content terminologies, developing social and academic English, learning a classroom culture that is different from their home culture, and a host of other issues such as a high rate of poverty and inequitable access to academic resources (LeClaire, Doll, Osborn, & Jones, 2009). Like others, we believe that if ELLs are to succeed in school they must receive highly motivating, rigorous instruction that supports the continuing development of their self-efficacy and their academic performance. Bouchey and Harter (2005) suggested that a student's self-efficacy is one of the most powerful predictors of academic performance. They explained that the relationship between self-efficacy and academic performance is consistent with Wigfield's (1994) expectancy value theory, which suggests that a student's expectations about his or her potential to do well on a particular task are compounded by the value the student places on the task. Although their study supported only the positive influence of students' self-efficacy on academic achievement, March, Trautwein, Lüdtke, Köller, and Baumert (2005) found a reciprocal relationship between students' self-efficacy and academic achievement. Therefore a student's success in a particular academic task contributes to his or her positive self-perception regarding the student's skill in regard to that task, though the contribution of self-perception to achievement, as well as to later self-perception, is stronger.

Because we believe that motivating instruction is the conduit that begins this self-perpetuated stream of success, we have designed these highly motivating, yet rigorous, text-based, scaffolded lessons. These lessons are specifically designed to enhance linguistic and literacy subskills that facilitate both ELLs' and mainstream students' acquisition of core curriculum knowledge. The national TESOL (Teachers of English to Speakers of Other Languages) English language proficiency standards (Gottlieb, Carnuccio, Ernst-Slavit, & Katz, 2006) and the English language arts Common Core Standards (2010) provide each lesson's standards base. Lessons are constructed to meet general grade-level proficiencies (K–8) while directly reflecting proficiencies that are commonly evaluated through language assessments such as those in the California English Language Development Test (CELDT), the Student Oral Language Observation Matrix (SOLOM), the Texas Essential Knowledge and Skills for Spanish Language Arts and English as a Second Language, the Second Language Proficiency Examination for Modern Languages of New York, as well as in Florida's Department of Education Curriculum Framework Providing English for Speakers of Other Languages (ESOL).

Organization and Management of the Strategy Lessons

Because language is an integration of linguistic, literacy, and cognitive skills, each lesson is categorized into one of the following areas to reflect its primary functional purpose as a base for oracy, reading, and writing: pronunciation, grammar, vocabulary, comprehension, and fluency. Lessons are also supported by student texts that can be used with an entire class or with a smaller group or an individual to introduce the concepts and the focus strategy and skills addressed in the lesson. Readings are coded as B (beginning), I (intermediate), or A (advanced). Introduced with Common Core and TESOL standards and a statement of purpose, each lesson is supported by research. Utilizing a gradual release-of-responsibility frame for instruction, each lesson also provides an example of modeling by the teacher, ideas for guided instruction and examples of supports that can be offered as students try on what the teacher has modeled (**Teacher Modeling and Guiding**). To facilitate additional time for intervention, ideas for **Peer Collaboration and Extension** follow. As the students participate in collaborative activities, three additional interventions are offered to support their various levels of proficiency (**Teacher Differentiating and Accommodating**). Oral language development is the focus for these three activities, which are also labeled beginning, intermediate, and advanced. **Tech It Out!**, a segment of each lesson, identifies a related technology connection. We caution you to have your students comply with your school's technology code of ethics. Related websites that support differentiated instruction are also included. Our intent in developing these lessons is to provide you with examples of rigorous, intentional, yet highly motivating instruction that are supportive of academic language and literacy growth for your ELLs. In the Appendix, **Teacher Resource A** allows teachers to record student needs and plan for intervention. **Teacher Resource B** lists suggested books by strategy lesson.

Continuous Assessment Informs Grouping and Instruction

As teachers, we realize that once a concept has been introduced to the entire class, small-group instruction must occur in order to accommodate students' performance differences. In an attempt to answer the question of what to do with the other students while you're working with a small group of students with similar strengths or needs, we have included lesson extensions for each lesson. This means that there are

25 base lessons and 75 extension lessons, grounded in scientifically based research-to-practice theories that support the belief that language is the process of conveying and receiving messages.

How Is Language Acquired and Developed?

Receiving and sharing information through language involves receptive and productive linguistic competence. Receptive competence is the knowledge or understanding of interactive conventions such as comprehending language visually or aurally. Productive competence is the ability to produce a wide range of language forms in communication, including conventional grammatical and syntactical structures. An added dimension of meaningful interaction is communicative competence, which involves using either productive or receptive skills and is defined as "the ability to use any form of language appropriate to the demands of social situations" (Harris & Hodges, 1995, p. 36). The lessons in this book are designed to develop literacy competence, which involves the ability to build on one's listening and oral skills while also developing reading and writing proficiencies.

Second-language learning involves the same processes that are employed in learning a first language. As we heard our first words, we identified and began to produce phonemic (sound) units. Through conversations with parents or other caregivers, we responded to directives and endeavored to express ourselves, at first with one- or two-word utterances (e.g., *mama, all gone, bye-bye*). Our productive efforts were increasingly enhanced as we connected morphological (grammatical) units, including prefixes (*inter-, re-, pre-, trans-*), suffixes (*-ing, -ful, -est, -able*) and root words (e.g., *play, catch*). In addition, we began to understand that the words we were hearing followed specific syntactic (ordered) patterns (e.g., *baby bye-bye* became *Baby go bye bye*; *Daddy home* became *Daddy is home*). As our lexicon (word knowledge) expanded, we learned the semantic (linguistically significant) information that helped us convey our intended messages. As a learner continues to communicatively interact with others, his or her scope of competence expands to encompass the area of pragmatics, in which the person understands the social dynamics—or interactions of formal and informal use, for example—of language (Salus & Flood, 2003).

Focusing on Forms

The following is a communicative exchange between Maria and her teacher that illustrates each type of linguistic formation. Notice how Maria's teacher guides and praises her efforts, thus promoting Maria's self-efficacy and potential for success.

TEACHER: Good morning, Maria. I see you brought the book *Too Many Tamales* [Soto, 1993] to school today. Let's talk about your book for a few minutes, all right?

MARIA: Okay.

TEACHER: Can you tell me the first sound in the word *tamales*?

Phonemic

MARIA: [producing the /t/ sound] "t."

TEACHER: Wonderful! [after reading, asks] What happens in the story? Didn't the young girl lose something?

Morphemic

MARIA: [demonstrating knowledge of the past tense of *lose*] She lost a ring.

TEACHER: Oh, I see. We will look forward to hearing about your story today during book talks. Now, will you please read this word for me [pointing to the word *Christmas*]?

Phonologic

MARIA: [Begins by producing the /ch/ sound.]

TEACHER: Yes, Maria, you're correct to try the "ch" sound, but here, the *ch* is pronounced like a *k*. It's like the *ch* in the word *chorus*.

MARIA: Christmas.

Syntactic

TEACHER: Terrific. Can you tell me, whom does the ring belong to? Is it the young girl's ring or is it the mother's ring?

MARIA: [noting the correct formation of the possessive] It's the mother's ring. The daughter loses it in the *masa*. It means dough.

TEACHER: Masa is the type of dough used for making tamales, isn't it?

Semantic

MARIA: Yes. At the end they find the ring.

TEACHER: I think the class is going to enjoy this story very much. Are you going to show the pictures as you talk about the story?

Pragmatic

MARIA: [demonstrating an understanding that visual representations might enhance a verbal description of the story] Yes. When I talk about the story I will show the pictures.

What Is the Theoretical Base for Language Learning?

Three main theories have influenced second-language instructional practices: the *behaviorist* theory, which was adapted from psychological studies; the *innatist* theory, which was based on studies in the field of linguistics; and the *interactionist* theory, which was derived from analysis of communicative exchanges between children and their caregivers. The negotiation of meaning has been found to be an integral element necessary for successful acquisition. The behaviorist view, developed by B. F. Skinner (1957), became prevalent after World War II. The theory, based on the hypothesis that we learn a second language through rote memorization, served as the catalyst for the audio-lingual approach, in which students memorize dialogues and practice verb forms and sentence structures. Through a stimulus–response method, the learner focuses on an object and repeats utterances modeled by the teacher. Behaviorists, however, could not resolve how learners generated novel formations they had never heard.

The innatist theory, primarily promoted by Chomsky (1969), purports that the learner is able to memorize, organize, and generalize rules. Chomsky believed that children universally possess an innate "grammar template" for attending to appropriate formations that enhance their communicative competency. This perspective is based on a premise that learners make generalizations about forms they observe and eventually refine their conceptualizations to accommodate irregularities in the language. After noticing that many verbs end with "ed" and are used to express the past tense, a child may declare, "I taked my money to the store." After more exposure to the irregular word *took*, the correct past-tense word form would be incorporated as part of the learner's stored knowledge of word formations.

The interactionist perspective, inspired by Krashen (1991, 2003), has been generally accepted among second-language theorists and practitioners who have highlighted it by focusing on the need for academic language interactions to occur within culturally responsive classrooms (González, Amanti, & Moll, 2008; O'Grady, 2008). Language engagement in school, according to Krashen's premises, must prepare the learner for real-life communication. In order to be linguistically proficient, students need to be able to express their thinking. Many scholars, including Cummins (2003) and Dutro (2008), suggest that without the ability to fluently converse using academic language, one's in-school potential, as well as later life potential for economic and personal growth, may be greatly constrained. This perspective illuminates the reality that sociocultural factors, such as the way a child feels his or her culture is valued in the classroom, certainly affects the child's self-efficacy and language learning (Au, 2007; Cummins, 2003; Nieto, 2005). Therefore, the classroom, which is one situation common to most children, needs to provide comprehensible language input and an environment that fosters conversational competence so that the student's knowledge expands through daily communicative situations.

What Is the Goal of This Book?

Drawing on the strengths of these theories, the primary goal of this book is to provide standards-related lessons and extensions that can enable you to accommodate the linguistic differences among your students through effective, developmentally scaffolded text-supported instruction that promotes intentional thinking between the reader and the ideas presented by the author in the text. All lessons are designed to support students as they construct ideas and language based on initial connections with texts shared by their teacher or read independently, ensuing conversations with their teacher and classmates about text, and analysis and evaluation of information found in texts.

References

Au, K. (2007). Culturally responsive instruction: Application to multiethnic classrooms. *Pedagogies*, 2(1), 1–18.

Bouchey, H., & Harter, S. (2005). Reflected appraisal, academic self-perceptions, and math/science performance during early adolescence. *Journal of Educational Psychology*, 97(4), 673–686.

Capps, R., Fix, M., Murray, J., Ost, J., Passel, J. S., & Herwantoro, S. (2005). *The new demography of America's schools: Immigration and the No Child Left Behind Act*. Washington DC: Urban Institute.

Chomsky, N. (1969). Should traditional grammar be ended or mended. *Education Review*, 22(1), 5–17.

Common Core State Standards Initiative. (2010). *Application for English language learners*. Retrieved December 17, 2010, from *www.corestandards.org/assets/application-for-english-learners.pdf*.

Cummins, J. (2003). Reading and the bilingual student: Fact and friction. In G. G. Garcia (Ed.), *English learners: Reaching the highest levels of English literacy* (pp. 2–23). Newark, DE: International Reading Association.

Dutro, S. (2008). *A focused approach to systematic ELD instruction* (2nd ed.). San Marcos, CA: E. L. Achieve.

Echevarría, J., Vogt, M. E., & Short, D. J. (2007). *Making content comprehensible for English learners: The SIOP model*. New York: Pearson.

Freeman, B., & Crawford, L. (2008). Creating a middle school mathematics curriculum for English-language learners. *Remedial and Special Education*, 29(1), 9–19.

Garcia, G. E., & Montavon, M. V. (2007). Making content-area instruction comprehensible for English language learners. In D. Lapp, J. Flood, & N. Farnan (Eds.), *Content area reading instruction: Strategies that work* (pp. 157–174). Mahwah, NJ: Erlbaum.

González, N., Amanti, C., & Moll, L. C. (2008). Case study: Using students' cultural resources in teaching. In A. Rosebery & B. Warren (Eds.), *Teaching science to English language learners* (pp. 99–102). Washington, DC: National Science Foundation.

Gottlieb, M., Carnuccio, L., Ernst-Slavit, G., & Katz, A. (Eds.). (2006). *Pre K–12 English language proficiency standards*. Alexandria, VA: TESOL, Inc.

Harris, T., & Hodges, R. (Eds.). (1995). *The literacy dictionary: The vocabulary of reading and writing*. Newark, DE: International Reading Association.

Kindler, A. (2002). *Survey of the states' limited English proficient students and available educational programs and services: 2000–2001 summary report*. Prepared for OELA by the National Clearinghouse for English Language Acquisition and Language Instruction Programs, Washington, DC.

Krashen, S. (1991). *Bilingual education: A focus on current research*. Washington, DC: National Clearinghouse for Bilingual Education.

Krashen, S. (2003). *Explorations in language acquisition and use*. Portsmouth, NH: Heinemann.

LeClaire, C., Doll, B., Osborn, A., & Jones, K. (2009). English language learners' and non-English language learners' perceptions of the classroom environment. *Psychology in the Schools, 46*(6), 568–577.

March, H., Trautwein, U., Lüdtke, O., Köller, O., & Baumert, J. (2005). Academic self-concept, interest, grades, and standardized test scores: Reciprocal effects model of causal ordering. *Child Development, 76*(2), 397–416.

National Center for Education Statistics. (2010). *The condition of education 2010* (NCES 2010-028). Retrieved November, 5, 2010, from *nces.ed.gov/fastfacts/display.asp?id=96*.

National Clearinghouse for English Language Acquisition. (2008). *ELL demographics by state*. Washington, DC: Author. Retrieved October 14, 2010, from *www.scribd.com/doc/28806554/English-Language-Learners-in-Next-Generation-Assessment-and-Accountability*.

Nieto, S. (2005). *The light in their eyes: Creating multicultural learning communities*. New York: Teachers College Press.

O'Grady, W. (2008). Innateness, universal grammar, and emergentism. *Lingua, 118*(4), 620–631.

Ovando, C. J., Collier, V. P., & Combs, M. C. (2003). *Bilingual and ESL classrooms: Teaching in multicultural contexts* (3rd ed.). Boston: McGraw Hill.

Salus, P., & Flood, J. (2003). *Language: A user's guide. What we say and why*. New York: Guilford Press.

Skinner, B. F. (1957). *Verbal behavior*. New York: Appleton Century Crofts.

Wigfield, A. (1994). Expectancy-value theory of achievement motivation: A developmental perspective. *Educational Psychology Review, 6*, 49–78.

Clues for Comprehension

Common Core Standard

Ask and answer questions about key details in a text read aloud, in information presented orally, or through other media.

TESOL Standard

Make inferences from cues in decontextualized text.

Focus skill: Comprehension
Secondary skill: Pronunciation

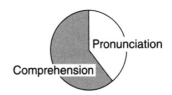

What Is the Purpose?

Use clues from the text to understand spoken and written language.

What Is the Research Base?

Listening to, discerning, and segmenting individual phonemes and meaningful units of sounds of the English language support language proficiency and comprehension (Cheung, 2009; Keller, Dalla Bella, & Koch, 2010). As students listen to sounds of their environment, and to the sounds of letters in words shared through language interactions, their awareness and appreciation of sounds and how these map to language is enhanced (Ericson & Juliebo, 1998). *Clues for Comprehension* offers ideas for engaging students in a conversation regarding words that have the same beginning sound (alliteration) and those with the same ending sound (rhyming) and thus enhances their understanding of the language base used for speaking and comprehending (Linklater, O'Connor, & Palardy, 2009).

Teacher Modeling and Guiding

1 The teacher begins the lesson by telling students that we become better readers by thinking about how letters, sounds, images, and words fit together to help us make meaning.

2 The teacher asks students to listen to the words in the text and creates related mental images to help them understand the story.

3 Using *The Little Old Lady Who Was Not Afraid of Anything* by Linda Williams as a mentor text, the teacher thinks aloud about the cover of the book: "I see a lady and a very large pumpkin. The cover of this book looks kind of spooky. I know authors use sounds to help me understand. I wonder what sounds I am going to hear in this book that will give me clues about what is happening."

4 In the first several pages the little old lady in the text comes across two shoes that go "clomp clomp." The teacher talk may include "Oh, these two shoes make the sound 'clomp clomp.' This sound will help me remember the spooky shoes." Displaying the chart shown as Work Page 1.1* the teacher says, "Let me draw a picture of the shoes and write the words that tell the sound they make, because this will help me remember the sound they made in the story."

5 After the teacher reads that the pants in the story go "wiggle wiggle" he or she might say, "These pants make this sound and I can picture pants in my mind wiggling like this [wiggles his or her hips]. I should always picture things in my mind to help me understand the words. What should I draw and write on my chart?"

6 After the students answer, the teacher continues. "Oh, here is a shirt. I bet it's going to also make a sound. I know this because the shoes made a sound and the pants made a sound. Let's see, what sound could a shirt make? Hmm. I bet something like 'shake shake.'"

7 The teacher continues thinking aloud while reading and completing the chart. The teacher remembers to include lots of "because statements" that explain the rationale for his or her thinking and also support students' understanding of their metacognition.

8 After reading three or four pages the teacher stops and asks the students to partner talk and answer questions such as (a) "What do you think is going to happen next?" or (b) "What sounds have we heard in this book so far? What will be the next sounds I draw and write on my chart?" While the students are turning to their partners and talking, the teacher should listen in to what they are saying.

---

* All reproducible Work Pages are at the ends of the respective chapters.

9 While listening, the teacher might guide the students with questions such as "Why do you think that?" or "What else might happen?" or "What clues from the text made you think that?" By guiding and assessing the students as they partner talk, the teacher can assess and support their comprehension. This information will help to plan subsequent interventions.

Peer Collaboration and Extension

1 During this time, students work in heterogeneous groups. Groups of students create their own versions of *The Little Old Lady Who Was Not Afraid of Anything*. Students use Work Page 1.1 for support as they write their versions of the text.

2 Using chart paper, these student groups use the mentor text as a guide as they fill in the columns shown in the chart below. Using the information they compiled on Work Page 1.1 and the chart below, they have support for comprehending and retelling their stories.

The Little Old Teacher Who Was Not Afraid of Anything

Object or person	Sound
Students	Chatter chatter
Pencils	Scribble scribble
Paper	Wrinkle wrinkle

3 As the students work, the teacher moves among them offering prompts and asking questions that support their performance. The teacher may say to partners who are having trouble creating a story with words and visuals, "What are you visualizing as you write your own version? The images you see in your mind are the ones you should draw on your chart; then write the words that describe the images. For example, when I drew the shoes on my chart, I also wrote the words *CLOMP CLOMP* to remind me of the sounds they made. That will help me understand what is happening in the story. What images can you draw on your chart to help you remember what story is about?"

4 The teacher also makes note of the similar needs existing among the students. This information will help him or her to offer later interventions to students with similar needs.

Teacher Differentiating and Accommodating

From the information the teacher gained as students worked collaboratively, he or she is now able to provide instruction that supports guided interventions for those with similar needs. Examples of this guided instruction are given in the following sections. As the teacher works with one group, others can be reading texts similar to those listed as suggested books or they can be engaged with the Tech It Out! activity (see below). They may also be illustrating and sharing with other groups their versions of *The Little Old Lady Who Was Not Afraid of Anything*.

Beginning Level

Students at the beginning level may not be able to identify sounds they hear. In order to explicitly teach particular sounds, the teacher has the students play Sound Bingo. Using a Bingo game format, students listen to a target sound made by the teacher, then find and cover the object/animal/nature sound pictured or displayed on their Bingo boards.

EXAMPLE

The teacher says "Meow." Each student covers a picture of a cat, using a Unifix cube, bean, or poker chip. Working in pairs, students check each other's answers. The game continues as the teacher says "Oink," "Quack," or "Moo." Students can win by having game pieces in rows across, up and down, diagonally, or by covering the entire board (blackout!). After the winning student shouts, "Bingo!," the student must "read" the pictures to assess whether he or she correctly matched each of the animals to its sound.

A variation of this activity is Letter–Sound Bingo. The teacher says a word, and if a student has a picture that matches the beginning sound of the teacher's word, a game piece can be placed down. A sample game board is shown in Example 1.1.

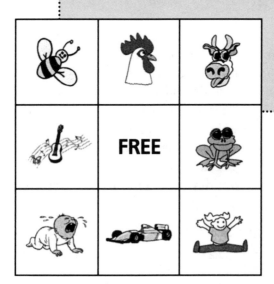

EXAMPLE 1.1. Sample game board.

Intermediate Level

Students working at the intermediate level can create a poem using words/sounds. Each successive line of the poem includes greater detail than the last. The teacher guides the students in understanding how listening to sounds provides an understanding for what they are reading. After students have created their poems, they can be shared with a small group or the whole class and listeners can be invited to "guess" the animal. When finished, students can draw an illustration to match the poem.

Meow!	Squeak!	Roar!
Loud meow	Soft squeak	Scary roar
Long, loud meow	Soft, quiet squeak	Scary, loud roar
Low, long, loud meow	High, soft, quiet squeak	Growly, scary, loud roar
(Cat)	(Mouse)	(Bear)

Advanced Level

Students at the advanced level might be listening to sounds that are often confused. For example, sounds such as /ee/, /ea/, and /ie/ can all have the long *e* sound. The teacher explicitly directs students to pay attention to letters that have similar sounds but different spellings. Students at this level can make a flip-strip Foldable® (see Example 1.2) to help with the confusion. Words are written on the outside flap, and definitions and sentences are written on the inside. Some possible confusing sounds to include are the following:

Sound	Spelling	Examples
Long *e*	ee, ea, ie	*free, streak, field*
Long *i*	y, ie, igh	*my, tie, night*
/aw/	augh, aw,	*taught, paw*

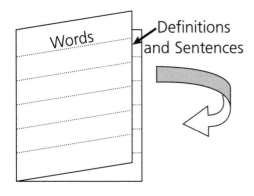

EXAMPLE 1.2. Flip-strip Foldable®.

Tech It Out!

The teacher creates an easy-to-use audio or video recording of sounds being taught. Students repeat sounds after seeing/hearing them on a monitor at a listening center, during a PowerPoint presentation, or through a KidPix presentation with added audio on a computer. This can be used as a center where students work collaboratively or with a teacher who is modeling and guiding the students in their work. KidPix can be used to artfully represent concepts presented in a text and to reinforce consonant or vowel sounds and overall reading fluency. Advanced teacher "techies" may wish to incorporate podcasting in any of their creative activities reflecting the text to present to a separate group or to a wider classroom audience (*www.mackiev.com/kid_pix. html*).

Suggested Websites and Books

www.earlyliterature.ecsd.net/resources1.htm
atozteacherstuff.com
www.learn4good.com/languages/index.htm
Dinahzikes.com

Anonymous—*A Treasury of Mother Goose Rhymes* (1984); Simon & Schuster.
Bunting, Eve—*So Far from the Sea* (2009); Sandpiper.
Lapsley, Arthur Brooks—*The Writings of Abraham Lincoln: Volume 2. 1843–1858* (2010); CreateSpace.
Lobel, Arnold—*On Market Street* (1989); Greenwillow Books.
Soto, Gary—*Chato and the Party Animals* (2004); Puffin.

References

Cheung, Y. K. (2009). *Phonological transcribing of English utterances in teaching listening comprehension for Korean students.* Available through ERIC Document Services (ED505326).

Ericson, L., & Juliebo, M. (1998). *The phonological awareness handbook for kindergarten and primary teachers.* Newark, DE: International Reading Association.

Keller, P., Dalla Bella, S., & Koch, I. (2010). Auditory imagery shapes movement timing and kinematics: Evidence from a musical task. *Journal of Experimental Psychology: Human Perception and Performance, 36*(2), 508–513.

Linklater, D., O'Connor, R., & Palardy, G. (2009). Kindergarten literacy assessment of English only and English language learner students: An examination of the predictive validity of three phonic awareness measures. *Journal of School Psychology, 47*(6), 369–394.

WORK PAGE 1.1

Pictures I See in My Mind When I Listen

Name: _____

Talking about Sounds and Words

Common Core Standard

Know and apply grade-level phonics and word analysis skills needed to decode and read words. Understand that as letters within words change, so do the sounds and the meanings (i.e., the alphabetic principle).

TESOL Standard

Identify graphic representations of sounds (e.g., letter combinations) contained in multicultural stories read by the teacher.

Focus skill: Pronunciation
Secondary skill: Comprehension

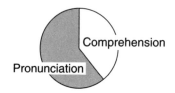

What Is the Purpose?

Identify phonemes and related letters in words to support gaining the meaning of words shared orally, through visuals, and in written text.

What Is the Research Base?

Understanding how to connect beginning, middle, and ending sounds to create words facilitates students' development of word knowledge, reinforces their understanding of sound–letter correspondence, and promotes transfer of linguistic principles from one language to another (Atwill, Blanchard, Christie, Corin, & Garcia, 2010; Pollard-Durodola & Simmons, 2009). The development of word knowledge is enhanced when visuals support word meaning (Vasquez, 2007). *Talking about*

Sounds and Words illustrates a five-step process that supports students learning to (1) pronounce, (2) label, (3) connect, (4) practice, and (5) read sound–letter combinations in words.

Teacher Modeling and Guiding

1 The teacher begins by talking about how sounds, letters, and words all connect to make meaning for us as we read.

2 Once a text has been selected for shared reading, words are identified for study and reproduced on colorful laminated word cards.

3 For example, after reading *The Cat in the Hat Comes Back* by Dr. Seuss, the teacher reviews the familiar three-phoneme letter patterns with the class using the laminated cards and the five-step process—(a) pronounce, (b) label, (c) connect, (d) practice, and (e) read—described in Example 2.1.

4 The teacher models how to complete Work Page 2.1 using two of the three selected words. He or she displays the Work Page on the document camera and writes *HAT* on the top line.

5 For example, the teacher may say, "A hat? Hmm. I wonder what that is used for in this story? I know that I wear a hat to keep the sun off my face. But that isn't

---

Hat

1. After pronouncing the word, the teacher can say, "*Hat*, let's repeat *hat*. This is a picture of a hat."
2. Next, the teacher asks the students how many letters are in the word *hat*.
3. Together, they say the name of each letter as the teacher identifies the letters one by one: "h-a-t."
4. The teacher says, "Each of these letters stands for a sound in the word." The teacher models the sound of each: /h/ letter *h*, /a/ letter *a*, /t/ letter *t*. Then the sounds are blended together to make a word. "Let's put these sounds together to read a word." (Repeat several times.)

Mat

1. After **pronouncing** the word, the teacher announces, "*Mat*, let's repeat *mat*. This is a picture of a mat."

(Repeat steps 2–5 for the word *mat*.)

Ran

1. After **pronouncing** the word, the teacher announces, "*Ran*, let's repeat *ran*. This is a picture of children who ran."

(Repeat steps 2–5 for the word *ran*.)

EXAMPLE 2.1. How a teacher can talk about words.

why the cat is wearing this hat. He's wearing a hat so that the other characters can recognize him."

6 Then the teacher draws a picture and uses the word in a sentence that is related to the book. For example, he or she may write, *The cat with his hat sat on the mat.*

7 Next, the teacher discusses the meaning, connecting it to the students' lives. The teacher may say, "Hmm, I have lots of hats. But none that look like the cat's."

8 Students are invited to talk about the meaning of *hat*, pronouncing the word and looking at the letters.

9 Students, each working with a partner, are asked to take turns pronouncing, labeling, connecting, practicing, and reading sound–letter combinations in the target words and those of their own.

Peer Collaboration and Extension

1 During this time, students work in heterogeneous groups.

2 Students choose three words from their independent reading books to pronounce, label, connect, practice, and read.

3 Using index cards, students draw and label each word and write a sentence using that word.

4 One of the goals of this activity is to get students to think about other words that share the phonemes being studied. So, for example, students can brainstorm a list of words that rhyme with the target word *hat* (e.g., *fat, bat, splat*).

5 Students punch a hole in the corner of each card, put a metal ring through, and then share their cards with other student groups. The metal ring keeps each student's cards grouped together and organized by rhyming words.

6 As the students work, the teacher moves among them offering prompts and asking questions that support their performance. Examples include, "Say that again. What sounds are you hearing? Say it slowly so you can hear the sounds." As the teacher supports pronunciation and comprehension, he or she also makes note of the similar needs existing among the students. This information can help the teacher to offer later interventions to students with similar needs. Examples of this follow.

Teacher Differentiating and Accommodating

From the information the teacher gained as students worked collaboratively, he or she is now able to offer instruction that provides guided interventions to those with similar needs. As the teacher does so, the others can be reading texts similar to those listed as suggested books, can be engaged with the Tech It Out! activity, or can be working with a partner to add to their list of rhyming words and practicing them in sentences.

Beginning Level

After a read-aloud or shared reading in a content area of study, students can brainstorm singular nouns, which are recorded by the teacher on a large piece of chart paper. Illustrations or pictures can be added to the chart to support emergent and early readers. Students sit in a circle, and one rolls a beach ball to a partner. Student 1 (rolling the ball) says a noun from the list and student 2 (receiving the ball) says the plural of student 1's noun. This will become more challenging as students learn, for example, that the plural version of *tooth* is *teeth*. A list of possible words can include *cat/cats, puppy/puppies, ear/ears, bunny/bunnies, bear/bears*. Words can be generated from a content area of study or a fictional text.

bee

fox

List of possible words:
cat/cats
puppy/puppies
ear/ears
bunny/bunnies
bear/bears

Words can be generated from a content area of study or the suggested books: *Corn Is Maize, The Cat in the Hat Comes Back, A World of Wonders, The Runaway Bunny,* and *Bears, Bears, and More Bears*

Intermediate Level

Students orally brainstorm a list of singular nouns after the teacher reads from an intermediate-level text (e.g., *Great Wonders of the World, Big Book of Dinosaurs*). The teacher records the nouns on large chart paper, including some nouns that do not change when pluralized (*moose*) and some irregular plural nouns (*foot/feet*). In pairs, students write the list of reordered singular nouns and add the plural counterparts. With their partners, students take turns orally creating sentences, first using the singular noun, and then the plural noun. Students can record three or four of their sentences on sentence strips or large charts with illustrations. Students share word lists and sentences within small groups or with the class.

The small *dinosaur* met two bigger *dinosaurs* at the watering hole.

Advanced Level

After the teacher has taught and reviewed the different types of nouns, a set of cards for sorting can be created (see Example 2.2). These cards should have common, proper, concrete, abstract, compound, and collective nouns. The students sort the nouns by their common properties. A picture of the noun can be added to a card for added support if needed. An excellent resource is Ruth Heller's *Merry-Go-Round* or *A Cache of Jewels*.

Using the teacher-prepared cards, the students perform a closed sort. Students place the noun cards in columns according to the type of noun. The teacher models this activity, having students place noun cards on a large prepared chart that is similar to individual word sort boards. Students can work in pairs or independently. If working in pairs, students can check with each other as they sort their noun cards.

Tech It Out!

Using a document camera or an overhead projector, the teacher displays letter tiles to form words and then projects them onto a screen. Students can manipulate the letter tiles, paying particular attention to prefixes and suffixes. Students can also sort word tiles according to parts of speech. Working in small groups, students should be encouraged to talk about the meanings of the words, prefixes, suffixes, and parts of speech and to use each word in a sentence. To sort words on a computer, try *www. readwritethink.org/materials/wordfamily*. Another way to integrate technology is for teachers to use audio or video recordings of words being taught. Students repeat the words after seeing/hearing them. For added visual stimulation these activities could be done using audio added to a PowerPoint presentation. As students become more proficient, their voices may be recorded on the PowerPoint presentation or in

Common	Proper	Concrete	Abstract	Compound	Collective
a pencil	King Arthur	apple	hope	countdown	BUNCH of bananas
a cat	Camelot	grapes	faith	horsefly	GAM of whales
a table	Principal Smith	oceans	love	cowboy	SCHOOL of fish

EXAMPLE 2.2. Noun sort.

a simple program such as KidPix. In addition, preparing these projects for other groups reinforces the skills of the students preparing the audio word project. This activity can also be used as students work in heterogeneous groups at centers/stations. See *www.kidpixcom.com.*

Suggested Websites and Books

breitlinks.com
www.childrenslit.com
www2.scholastic.co.uk/isbc

Aliki—*Corn Is Maize* (1986); Collins.
Brown, Margaret W.—*The Runaway Bunny* (2005); HarperCollins.
Geisel, Theodor S.—*The Cat In The Hat Comes Back* (1958); Random House.
Lewis, Patrick, J., and Joy, Alison—*A World of Wonders* (2002); Dial.
Naylor, Phyllis Reynolds—*Shiloh* (2000); Atheneum.
Park, Linda Sue—*Bee-Bim Bop!* (2009); Sandpiper.
Torres, Leyla—*Liliana's Grandmothers* (2005); Houghton Mifflin.
Wilson, Karma—*Bears, Bears, and More Bears* (2003); M. K. McElderry.
Wright, Blanche Fisher—*Original Mother Goose* (1992); Running Press Kids.
Wyndham, Robert—*Chinese Mother Goose Rhymes* (1998); Putnam Juvenile.

References

Atwill, K., Blanchard, J., Christie, J., Corin, J., & Garcia, H. (2010). English language learners: Implications of limited vocabulary for cross-language transfer of phonemic awareness with kindergartners. *Journal of Hispanic Higher Education*, 9(2), 104–129.

Pollard-Durodola, S., & Simmons, D. (2009). The role of explicit instruction and instructional design in promoting phonemic awareness development and transfer from Spanish to English. *Reading and Writing Quarterly*, 25(2–3), 139–161.

Vasquez, V. (2007). Using the everyday to engage in critical literacies with young children. *New England Reading Association Journal*, 43(2), 6–12.

Talking about Words

Name: _____

Word: _____

1. _____
_____
_____
_____

Word: _____

2. _____
_____
_____
_____

Sounding Out Words for Reading

Common Core Standard

Know and identify sound–spelling correspondences and use these to decode words

TESOL Standard

Practice saying illustrated word pairs.

Focus skill: Pronunciation
Secondary skill: Comprehension

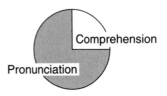

Comprehension

Pronunciation

What Is the Purpose?

Identify the beginning, middle, and ending sounds in words.

What Is the Research Base?

Developing a familiarity with the names of letters, the sounds represented by letters in words, and word meanings are essential components of reading (McKenna, Walpole, & Conradi, 2010). One's facility with visual and orthographic patterns in words, phonological awareness, and fluency supports reading comprehension (McGee & Richgels, 2007; Stahl, Dougherty, & McKenna, 2006). Much intentional practiced repetition is needed for English learners to gain proficiency with phonemic awareness and fluency and to use these to support their comprehension. *Sounding Out Words for Reading* provides opportunities for students to expand their understanding of word meanings and gain independence as readers by pronouncing, labeling, connecting, practicing, and reading context-supported sound–letter combinations in words.

Teacher Modeling and Guiding

1 The teacher begins the lesson by telling students that we become better readers by thinking about the position of sounds in words. He or she explains that when we can read these quickly, we are better able to understand the story. The teacher should model his or her thinking in the following way: "All words are made up of sounds. There are sounds at the beginning of words, in the middle of words, and at the end. Let's think about my last name, *West*. At the beginning I hear /w/. In the middle I hear /e/, and at the end I hear /st/. By listening to the beginning, middle, and end of a word I can think about the letters that go with the sounds. Sometimes there is one letter that represents the sound and at other times, as in my name (*st*), letters blend to make the sound. Let's listen again." The teacher holds up his or her fingers, one at a time, in order to show the students more concretely how sounds map to letters and which ones are in his or her name.

2 The teacher models sound–letter correspondences in a few additional one-syllable words and student names (*cat, Kim, school, day*) and then asks students to turn to a partner and try identifying the letters and sounds in their own last names and other words they select.

3 As pairs of students are working, the teacher listens in to assess and guide their thinking. Prompts such as "Say that again" or "Does that sound come at the beginning of the word or the end of the word?" may be helpful.

4 For more proficient students, multisyllabic words can be used. In the case of the word *butterfly*, they identify the beginning, middle, and ending sound of each syllable (/but/, /ter/, /fly/).

5 Example 3.1. offers more examples.

6 The teacher models how to fill out Work Page 3.1 by thinking aloud about sounds heard at the beginning, middle, and end of words. The teacher should select words that are being studied as part of a word study experience in spelling or in the students' content area reading.

Before modeling each segment, the teacher lists the target words so the students can view them as they are discussed.

A. Teacher says (modeling the sounds): I see the letter(s):	**Students listen, see, and say the letter:**
1. *p* in the word *pond*. (onset)	p
2. *br* in the word *breeze*. (blend)	br
3. *str* in the word *stretch*. (blend)	str
4. *r* in the word *clear*. (last consonant)	r
5. *t* in the word *water*. (middle consonant)	t

B. The teacher says and writes: What is a word that … ?	**Student listens, sees, and says the sounds:**
1. begins with the sound /t/ as in the word *tell*.	tail
2. ends with the sound /z/, but is spelled with an *se* as in the words *cheese* and *please*.	ease
3. contains the sound /m/ as in the word *camel*.	animals

C. The teacher says and writes: What is a word that shares this letter pattern?	**Students listen, see, and say the word *chunk*:**
1. *ight* as in the word *sight*. (vowel and last sound of a word, a rime)	might
2. *qu* as in *quiet*. (onset)	quick
3. *ph* as in the word *photography*. (digraph)	telephone

D. The teacher says and writes: What is a word that … ?	**Student listens, sees, and says the rhyming words:**
1. rhymes with the word *city*?	kitty
2. rhymes with the word *house*?	mouse
3. rhymes with the word *crop*?	hop
4. rhymes with the word *grow*?	show

E. The teacher asks, when you see this word what definition do you think of?	**Student listens, sees, reads, and writes definitions:**
1. community	A place where people live, work, and have fun together
2. urban	Living in a city
3. rural	Living on a farm

EXAMPLE 3.1. Sounding out words.

Peer Collaboration and Extension

1 During this time, students are working in heterogeneous groups. As they work, the teacher moves among them offering prompts and asking questions that support their performance. He or she also makes note of the similar needs existing among the students. This information can help the teacher to offer later interventions to students with similar needs.

2 Each group of students segments words of their choice for a game to play against another group.

3 Using Work Page 3.2, students fill in their mystery words to later be guessed by another group.

4 Once the chart is completed, each group joins another group, orally says each part of the word, and their opponents try to guess the word.

5 For an additional challenge the groups may want to say the ending sounds first, then the middle sounds, then the beginning sounds, to see if they can stump their opponents (/k/, /i/ /tr/ = *trick*).

Teacher Differentiating and Accommodating

From the information the teacher gained as students worked collaboratively, he or she is now able to offer instruction that provides guided interventions to students with similar needs. As the teacher does so, the other students can read texts similar to those listed as suggested books, or they can be engaged with the Tech It Out! activity or continue to work on the mystery word chart.

Beginning Level

Using predetermined individual letters written on a large piece of paper, students physically create two-, three-, four-, and five-letter words (Cunningham & Hall, 1994). As the words are created, students orally say the letters and sounds, creating the words. At the culmination of this activity, a mystery word is physically created from all the letters.

> **EXAMPLE: Use the letters *i, a, o, d, s, n, r,* and *u***
>
> Two-letter words—*is, in, no, on, do, us*
> Three-letter words—*sun, run, ran, Dan, and, sad, rod, sod, nod*
> Five-letter words—*dinos, round, sound*
>
> The mystery word is *dinosaur.* As the mystery word is created, the students orally share the word with their partners, stating the word in a sentence for meaning. Words can also be generated from a beginning-level text, such as *Animal ABC.*

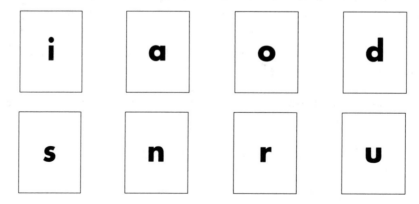

Intermediate Level

Using the same format of *Making Words* (Cunningham & Hall, 1994), with predetermined letters written by the teacher on large construction paper, students physically create three-, four-, and five-letter words that have blends and digraphs. Working with a partner, students can use the words orally in a sentence for meaning. The culmination of this activity is a predetermined mystery word formed from all the letters. A suggested book for the intermediate level is *The Midnight Ride of Paul Revere* (Longfellow, 2001).

> **EXAMPLE: Use the letters *h, i, d, o, m, n, g, t,* and *i***
>
> Three-letter words—*hid, mid, Tom, Tim, dig, dog*
>
> Four-letter words—*thin, ting, ding, nigh*
>
> Five-letter words—*might, night*
>
> The mystery word is *midnight*. As the mystery word is created, the students orally share the word with their partners, stating the word in a sentence to clarify its meaning.

Advanced Level

Using the same format *Making Words* (Cunningham & Hall, 1994), with letters written by the teacher on a large piece of paper, students physically create three-, four-, and five-letter words that have prefixes and suffixes. Each working with a partner, students can use the words orally in a sentence for meaning. Discovering a predetermined mystery word is the culmination of this activity.

> **EXAMPLE: Use the letters *e, i, u, g, n n, p,* and *s***
>
> Three-letter words—*pin, pen, peg, pig*
>
> Four-letter words—*pigs, pins, pens, pine*
>
> Five-letter words—*unpin, sing, spine*
>
> The mystery word is *penguins*. As the mystery word is created, the students orally share the word with their partners and tell a story about the subject of the mystery word (penguins).

Tech It Out!

Using software such as Living Books and various websites with audio clips, students can listen to words and stories being read. By clicking on the microphone icon, students can hear the pronunciation of words, different languages, and songs. There are several websites where students can listen to stories, interact with characters, and play educational games. Try *pbskids.org* and *www.rif.org/readingplanet/content/*

read_aloud_stories.mspx. Another way the teacher can reinforce this strategy is to create easy-to-use recordings of words being sounded out. Students can repeat the words as they are heard. This audio extension of Strategy Lesson 3 can be used as students work at independent learning centers in the classroom. Teachers can also use Bailey's Book House or other Living Books software to reinforce the strategy of sounding out words. They can see *www.k12software.com* and compile a list of valuable audio technology resources for the classroom.

Suggested Websites and Books

www.readingrockets.org/shows/launching/sounds
eslus.com/eslcenter.htm
www.corestandards.org/the-standards/

English, Karen—*Nadia's Hands* (2009); Boyds Mills Press.
Hamanaka, Sheila—*All the Colors of the Earth* (1999); HarperCollins.
hooks, bell—*Homemade Love* (2002); Hyperion Books for Children.
Hadaway, Nancy L.—*Breaking Boundaries with Global Literature: Celebrating Diversity in K–12 Classrooms* (2007); International Reading Association.
Piper, Watty—*The Little Engine That Could* (1990); Grosset & Dunlap.

References

Cunningham, P. M., & Hall, D. P. (1994). *Making Words.* Carthage, IL: Good Apple.

McGee, L. M., & Richgels, D. J. (2007). *Literacy beginnings: Supporting young readers and writers* (5th ed.). Boston: Allyn & Bacon.

McKenna, M. C., Walpole, S., & Conradi, K. (Eds.). (2010). (Eds.) *Promoting early reading: Research, resources, and best practices.* New York: Guilford Press.

Stahl, K., Dougherty, E., & McKenna, M. C. (Eds.). (2006). *Reading research at work: Foundations of effective practice.* New York: Guilford Press.

Sounding Out Words

Name: _____

My Word	Beginning Sound	Middle Sound	End Sound

Mystery Words

Name: _____

Beginning Sound	Middle Sound	End Sound	Guess My Word?
/b/	/oo/	/k/	book
/tr/	/ay/	/n/	train
/extra/	/ordin/	/ary/	extraordinary

Choral Reading

Common Core Standard

Read with sufficient accuracy and fluency to support comprehension.

TESOL Standard

Replicate sounds through gestures, stress and intonation, patterns of rhymes, prose or poetry with a partner.

Focus skill: Fluency
Secondary skill: Comprehension

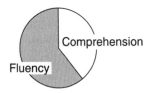

What Is the Purpose?

Chorally read a text with fluency.

What Is the Research Base?

Reading aloud improves readers' intonation, diction, phonological awareness, and oral fluency (Mesmer & Lake, 2010). Engaging in oral practice with a proficient model can help students discern all sounds presented within a word (Xu, 2010). Listening to and reading patterned poetry, with predictable sentence structures, enables language learners to focus on vocabulary and the meaning contained in the messages (McQuillan, 2009). *Choral Reading* provides opportunities for students to analyze the linguistic and conceptual meanings represented by written and spoken language they can read.

Teacher Modeling and Guiding

1 Prior to the lesson the teacher writes a poem on chart paper large enough for all students to see. Another option is to make a copy for each student.

2 The teacher reads the poem out loud. The poem in Example 4.1 works well for this strategy.

3 The teacher encourages students to listen carefully to how he or she reads smoothly, not like a robot would.

4 After modeling fluent reading the teacher reads word by word and thinks aloud for the students. The teacher may say, "This sounds very choppy. When I read like this I am slow and I sound like a robot. It is hard for listeners to understand my words and what the words mean. I also have a hard time understanding the meaning of what I am reading."

5 The teacher invites students to partner talk about his or her disfluent, choppy reading. The teacher listens in as the students share comments about the reading and mimic the teacher. The teacher may need to guide students to understand that fluent reading means reading at a pace that allows one to comprehend. The teacher also emphasizes that it does not mean just reading fast.

6 For a second reading of the poem, the teacher invites students to chorally read with him or her. The teacher explains that, when we read together, we must read at a steady pace.

7 As students become more confident with their reading, they join in with the others.

8 After reading the target text, the teacher models how to fill out Work Page 4.1. The teacher should remember to model how good readers and writers reread text often. "The more we read something, the smoother we sound. We won't sound like robots now."

9 After writing his or her own version of the Mike, Matt, and Mia poem, the teacher illustrates it.

10 The teacher invites students to talk in pairs about the words they may use when writing their own versions of this poem.

> **Friends**
>
> Mike and Matt and Mia, too.
> So many things that we can do.
> We can dance and we can skip
> On our way to the zoo.
>
> We can run and we can play.
> Laughing and singing every day
> We can jump and we can hop
> Playing hopscotch along the way.
>
> What, you ask, are friends to me?
> Someone to share, explore, and dream.
> Like rays of sun that warm my heart
> Mike, Matt, and Mia, how friends should be.

EXAMPLE 4.1. Sample poem.

Peer Collaboration and Extension

1 During this time, students are working in heterogeneous groups to create their own poems, using Work Page 4.1.

2 As the students work, the teacher moves among them, offering prompts and asking questions that support their performance. "Good readers reread often. Please reread this line of your poem for me. This time, read it together in a group. See how more fluent you sound when you reread text. This will help with your comprehension too!" She also makes note of the similar needs existing among the students. This information helps the teacher to offer later interventions to students with similar needs.

3 After the groups write their own versions of the poem, they should practice them several times. The teacher may want to allow for some time at the end of the lesson to have groups of students recite their poems.

Teacher Differentiating and Accommodating

From the information the teacher gained as students worked collaboratively, he or she is able to provide instruction that supports guided interventions to students with similar needs. As he or she does so, the others can be reading texts similar to those listed as suggested books or can be engaged with the Tech It Out! activity. If they have not finished practicing or sharing their poems, they can continue doing so.

Beginning Level

Students begin by listening to the teacher read aloud a poem from a book at the beginning level (e.g., *101 Science Poems & Songs for Young Learners*). The students listen for fluency, expression, intonation, and proper word pronunciation. The poem or song can be rewritten on chart paper for all students to see. The students chorally read and perform the poem as a group or with a partner using total physical response (TPR) during their parts; that is, they use gestures and movements to act out certain parts of their poem.

Intermediate Level

Selecting a Reader's Theatre script from *www.teachingheart.net/readerstheater.htm*, the teacher does a small group shared reading modeling fluency, expression, intonation, and proper word pronunciation. Students rehearse and perform the Reader's Theatre with partners or in small groups. During the rehearsal period, the teacher visits each group and helps students with tricky words and confusing phrasing.

Advanced Level

In partners, students create their own Reader's Theatre script based on current classroom literature or an informational text. A suggested book from the advanced level (*Robert Frost's Poems*) can be used as a basis for the script, or *www.lisablau.com/freescripts.html* can be visited for script ideas. Students rehearse their scripts several times before performing in front of other groups.

Tech It Out!

Incorporating music and lyrics is a great way to get students attending to print. Students usually love to sing along with the words, either by themselves or with a partner. Karaoke has never been the same! Check out *www.ksolo.com/join.do* and *eflclassroom.ning.com/index.php.* Another way to reinforce choral reading with students is to create easy-to-use recordings of a story being read. Students can read into the recorder and listen. More proficient students can record themselves reading into a recorder for less proficient students. A technology center for this activity would work well, as students can hear fluent reading and oral language can be developed through conversations about the story being listened to or read. Online reading programs such as Bailey's Book House, Millie's Math House, Sammy's Science House, and Trudy's Time and Place House may be used to help reinforce the strategy of choral reading online. Those interested in investigating this resource further can, visit *www.k12software.com.*

Suggested Websites and Books

www.prenhall.com
wwww.colorincolorado.org
www.english-to-go.com

Dahl, Roald—*Charlie and the Chocolate Factory* (2007); Puffin.
Grimes, Nikki—*Come Sunday* (1996); Eerdmans Books for Young Readers.
Hays, Anna Jane—*So Big!* (2003); Random House Books for Young Readers.
Perez, L. King—*First Day in Grapes* (2002); Lee & Low Books.
Schachner, Judy—*Skippyjon Jones in Mummy Trouble* (2008); Puffin.

References

McQuillan, K. (2009). Teachers reading aloud. *Principal Leadership, 9*(9), 30–31.
Mesmer, H., & Lake, K. (2010). The role of syllable awareness and syllable-controlled text in the development of finger-point reading. *Reading Psychology, 31*(2), 176–201.
Xu, S. H. (2010). *Teaching English language learners: Literacy strategies and resources for K–6.* New York: Guilford Press.

Picture the Poem

Name: _____

```




```
(Draw a picture here.)

Friends

Mike and Matt and Mia,_____.

So many things that_____.

We can dance and_____

on our way to the_____.

We can _____ and we can _____.

Laughing and _____ every _____.

We can _____ and we can_____

playing hopscotch along the _____.

What, you ask, are _____ to me?

Someone to share, _____, and dream.

Like _____ of _____ that warm my _____

Mike, Matt, and Mia, how _____ should be.

Talking about Visuals

Common Core Standard
Use information gained from illustrations and words in a print or digital text to demonstrate understanding of characters, setting, plot, or information.

TESOL Standard
Use context clues with graphically and visually supported text with a partner to construct meaning.

Focus skill: Vocabulary
Secondary skill: Comprehension

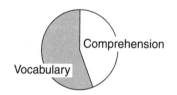

What Is the Purpose?

Use visuals to support understanding and conversation about texts.

What Is the Research Base?

Visual images provide context for learners as they attempt to associate images with words they encounter in texts (Pozzer-Ardenghi & Roth, 2010). Students draw from their personal language bases to describe visuals shown through illustrations or photographs (McLaughlin & Allen, 2009; Villano, 2005). When a concept is made visible, a student readily uses organizational strategies to categorize the new information within his or her existing semantic and associative clusters. *Talking about Visuals* illustrates how using visual supports provides students with authentic contexts through which language can be produced.

Teacher Modeling and Guiding

1 The teacher begins the lesson by showing the students the cover of a book, such as *The Recess Queen* (O'neill, 2002).

2 The teacher then thinks aloud by saying something such as "Wow! I can tell a lot about this book already by looking at the pictures. Even before I begin reading words, I can see that visual information tells me a lot."

3 The teacher continues this thinking throughout the text: "I know that the kids in this book are scared. Just look at their faces. The author doesn't tell me that but I can see it by looking at their faces."

4 As the teacher reads, he or she pauses to ask the students questions that cue them to think about the visual information—for example, "How do you think this makes the teacher feel?"; "What do you think the mom might be feeling?"; "How do you know?"

5 While students partner to discuss the questions, the teacher listens to their responses and supports students who are not attending to the pictorial information, with cues such as "Let's look at this picture again. What do you see?"

6 Once the text has been read aloud, the teacher should reiterate how visual information can sometimes give the reader much (or more) information in addition to the words an author uses. "That's why authors *and* illustrators are so important. Both give us clues to understanding what we read."

7 To reinforce the idea that visual information gives us clues to reading, the teacher models Work Page 5.1 for the students.

8 The teacher can say, "As I look at this form I can see that I need to add the source and page number of the picture I want to describe. These are important to include so I can show evidence of my work. It's a good idea to get in the habit of having this proof from the text I am working from."

9 Next the teacher can say, "As I look at the picture I selected, I am thinking of words to describe this picture. I will list these words here." (Teacher points to lines 1–10.)

10 The teacher invites students to talk in pairs about other possible words that could be listed on the lines. As the students talk, the teacher listens in to check that students are attending to the visual information the illustrator has provided in the book. The teacher may need to revisit some of the prompts used at the beginning of the lesson.

11 Next the teacher models for students how to use these descriptive words in sentences. Again, students are invited to brainstorm possible sentences that match the illustration being examined.

Peer Collaboration and Extension

1 During this time, students work in heterogeneous groups.

2 On a piece of paper, each student quickly sketches a picture.

3 Each student passes his or her paper to the student seated to the left.

4 This student writes one sentence to describe what he or she sees in the sketch.

5 When a sentence has been written, the students pass their papers again adding a new sentence each time.

6 After each of the students has added a sentence to the picture, they read their "story" out loud to see if what they wrote matches the sketch.

7 Students can pass papers around twice for a more detailed story. To support students, the teacher may wish to share a Vocabulary Tool Box similar to the one shown in Example 5.1. A blank version you can use is provided in Work Page 5.2.

8 As they work, the teacher moves among the students, offering cues and prompts and asking questions that support their performance. "I see you added one word that describes the picture. What else do you see? Good readers need to think about the words *and* pictures to understand what they read." The teacher also makes note of the similar needs existing among the students. This information can help him or her to offer later interventions to students with similar needs.

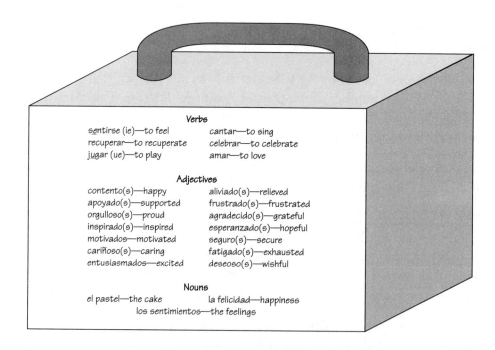

EXAMPLE 5.1. Completed Work Page 5.2.

Teacher Differentiating and Accommodating

From the information the teacher gained as students worked collaboratively, he or she is now able to often instruction that provides guided interventions to students with similar needs. As the teacher does so, the others can read texts similar to those listed as suggested books, they can be engaged with the Tech It Out! activity, or they can continue creating pictures and adding supportive language.

Beginning Level

Using a large picture (e.g., firefighters putting out a blazing fire), the teacher helps the students brainstorm vocabulary. "Tell me what you see in the picture," the teacher might say. The teacher records the vocabulary words on sticky notes and places them on the large picture. Using the brainstormed vocabulary, the teacher asks specific questions for the students to answer—for example: "What do the firefighters need to wear on their heads to protect them? This hat is called a *helmet*. Firefighters need to wear a helmet." It is important for teachers to build on the words students already know and generate vocabulary that is unique to their spoken and written vocabularies. For example, because students may know the word *hat*, the teacher should introduce the word *helmet* as a special kind of hat. Questioning and answering in complete sentences is modeled by the teacher in a "Busy Bees" activity. Students are then labeled as "bees" or "hives." When directed by the teacher, all students fly around to find a bee–hive pair. The teacher models a question/answer from the targeted picture prompt and then gives the hive student an opportunity to ask the bee student the same question that was modeled by the teacher. The bee student answers the question in a complete sentence, using the vocabulary generated from the large visual. Roles are switched, and the bee student asks the hive student the question and listens for an appropriate response. The process is repeated several times, using the same question until the teacher is satisfied. After Busy Bees all students regroup and create one sentence about the visual, using the generated vocabulary.

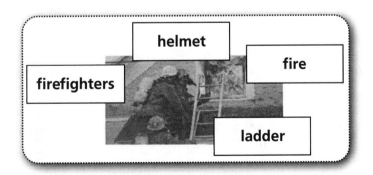

Teacher question: Why are the firefighters climbing up the ladder?

Class-generated written response:

> The firefighters are climbing up the ladder to put out the fire.

Intermediate Level

Using a large picture, such as two children in a park, students brainstorm vocabulary with the teacher. The teacher records vocabulary words on sticky notes and adds them to the picture (same as in the beginning-level strategy). Students are arranged in two circles, with the outside circle facing the inside circle, thus forming partners. The teacher models questioning and answering in complete sentences. Using the vocabulary generated from the picture, each student thinks up one question to ask his or her partner. The teacher decides if the outside or the inside circle asks a question first. After the questioning and answering, the students reverse their questioner–responder roles. After each student has had a chance to ask and respond to a question, the outside circle moves one person to the left and the process is repeated to the teacher's satisfaction. After the inside–outside circle activity is completed, the students independently write one or two sentences about the visual, using the generated vocabulary and questions and responses heard during the circle time.

Teacher-modeled question and answer: Why are the girls smiling? The girls are smiling because they read about something funny that happened in their book.

Possible student-generated questions: Why are the girls both wearing blue shirts and red pants? Where are the girls?

Possible sentence created:

> The two girls are smiling about something funny they read.

Advanced Level

As partners, students generate vocabulary from a large picture (e.g., a bicycle race) and list the words on a large chart. Students are encouraged to describe the picture using vocabulary in the context of "what happened before, what is happening now, and what will happen next" (past, present, future). Students share their descriptions with the class, using complete sentences and target words such as *before*, *during*, and *after*. This is a great way to help students summarize pictures as they "retell" what is happening.

bicycles
rides
helmets
fast
pavement
speeding
scorching
race

Possible sentences:

Before this bicycle race started, the racers needed to put on their helmets. *During* the race, the bicyclists rode fast along the scorching pavement. *After* the race, the riders needed to drink cold water from their water bottles.

Tech It Out!

Teachers and students take photos of their classroom and school environments using a digital camera. Photos are uploaded to the computer or printed. Small groups of students have a discussion about what they see in each photo. If taking pictures is not an option, students can look online for some interesting images and photos. A website that has particularly interesting photos and images is *www.nationalgeographic.com/kids*. Another way for the teacher to get students talking about visuals is to divide them into small groups. The teacher asks each group to create a scene that tells a story and has them take a digital picture. The groups then exchange digital pictures and write descriptions of what they think might be happening. The groups' stories can be compared. These can be compiled into an electronic slide show by using Apple's Keynote Presentation Software, Microsoft PowerPoint, or a similar program.

> ### *Suggested Websites and Books*
>
> *www.epals.com*
> *www.everythingesl.net*
> *np.harlan.k12.ia.us/ELL.htm*
>
> Baum, L. Frank—*The Wizard of Oz* (2008); Puffin.
> O'neill, Alexis—*The Recess Queen* (2002); Scholastic Press.
> Sheth, Kashmira—*Monsoon Afternoon* (2008); Peachtree Publishers.
> Williams, Karen Lynn—*Four Feet, Two Sandals* (2007); Eerdmans Books for Young Readers.
> Woodson, Jacqueline—*The Other Side* (2001); Putnam Juvenile.

References

McLaughlin, M., & Allen, M. (2009). *Guided comprehension in grades 3–8* (2nd ed.). Newark, DE: International Reading Association.

Pozzer-Ardenghi, L., & Roth, W. (2010). Toward a social practice perspective on the work of reading inscriptions in science texts. *Reading Psychology, 31*(3), 228–253.

Villano, T. L. (2005). Should social studies textbooks become history?: A look at alternative methods to activate schema in the intermediate classroom. *The Reading Teacher, 59*, 122–130.

WORK PAGE 5.1

Describing Pictures

Name: _____

Source and Page Number of Picture: _____

Words That Describe My Picture

1. _____   6. _____

2. _____   7. _____

3. _____   8. _____

4. _____   9. _____

5. _____   10. _____

Sentences Describing My Picture

_____

_____

_____

_____

_____

_____

_____

_____

_____

_____

_____

_____

_____

_____

_____

Vocabulary Tool Box

Name: _____

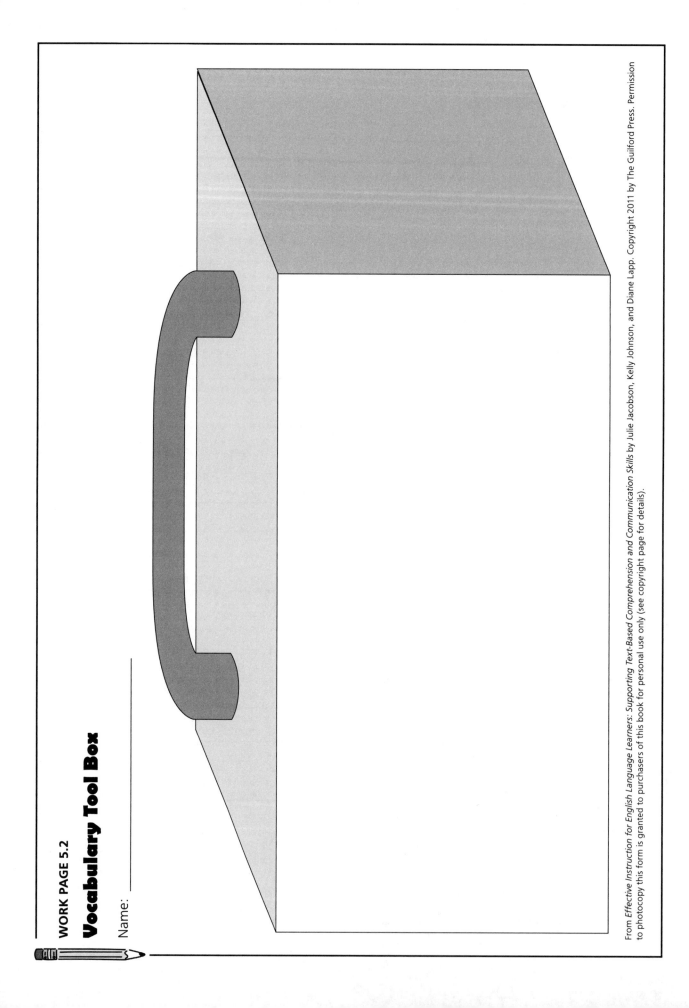

Role Play with Realia

Common Core Standard

Use related realia, illustrations, and details in a story to describe its characters, setting, or events.

TESOL Standard

Identify realia or objects in pictures in books from oral descriptions offered by teachers or other adults (e.g., pointing to the sentence "Brown bear, brown bear" in a book of the same title by Bill Martin, Jr. (1967): Holt).

Focus skill: Pronunciation
Secondary skill: Vocabulary

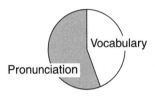

What Is the Purpose?

Use objects to dramatize a scene presenting problem and solution.

What Is the Research Base?

Drama provides a forum for presenting an integrated approach to language acquisition by engaging learners physically, emotionally, and cognitively in the language learning process (Greenwood & Flanigan, 2007; Kornfeld & Leyden, 2005). Words and grammatical formations of language are most readily retained in memory through meaningful, authentic, purposeful communication (Zehr, 2010). **_Role Play with Realia_** provides opportunities for students' ideas, thoughts, and feelings to be represented through concrete, visual methods as they engage in dramatic play.

Teacher Modeling and Guiding

1 The text that can be used for this strategy is a grade-appropriate scenario, including a list of related vocabulary words, depicting problems that may occur in everyday life, like the one in Example 6.1.

2 The teacher displays the scenario and vocabulary words on a document camera and reads the paragraph aloud. The teacher models how he or she might develop a logical solution to the problem. "Let's see. The problem here is that I am torn between hanging out with my friend and babysitting with my sister. I made a promise to my sister, but I really want to be with my friend. I wish I could do both but they are happening at the same times."

3 The teacher may want to add some props to this scenario, like a makeshift movie ticket, a photo of the sister, and a wristwatch.

4 The teacher may invite students to be part of the scene in which the teacher and students act out a solution to the problem. See Example 6.2. (*Note*: The teacher should choose students who feel comfortable doing this and who have worked ahead of time on solving the problem in the scenario.)

5 The realia are used to support the students' understanding of the problem and solution.

6 After the model skit has been performed in front of the class, the teacher and participating students write a short script to accompany their skit. The teacher may need to take the lead as he or she models the written format of a play/skit. The par-

My best friend invited me to go to the movies after school on Friday. I have already promised my sister that I would help her babysit neighborhood children who live on our block. I would like to go to the movies, but I don't want to disappoint my sister. What can I do?

la vecindad—the neighborhood	ayudar—to help
ir al cine—to go to the movies	Yo ya prometí—I already promised.
después—after	Sí puedo/No puedo—Yes I can/No I can't.
hasta—until	Empieza a las cinco—It begins at 5:00.
la película—the movie	Tengo una idea—I have an idea.
Yo he prometido—I have promised	Nuestros vecinos—our neighbors
Te gustaría—Would you like?	cuidar de los niños—to babysit
frustrar, desilusionar—to frustrate, disappoint	

EXAMPLE 6.1. Problem.

Dora:	Hi, Melissa. How are you?
Melissa:	Okay, I'm on my way to help my sister babysit some of the children in our neighborhood.
Dora:	Oh, really? I wanted to invite you to see the Disney movie *The Jungle Book*.
Melissa:	Oh Dora, thank you very much. I want to see that movie, but it might make my sister sad if I don't help her babysit.
Dora:	That's all right. I understand. We can go later. It will be at the theater for a long time.
Melissa:	I have an idea. Do you want to come and babyist the kids with us? We usually have a good time. The children behave well and are a lot of fun. We can go to see the move together next week.
Dora:	That sounds like a great idea. I'll call my mom and then I'll tell you if I can come after school.
Melissa:	Okay, I'll see you then. Bye, Dora!
Dora:	Good-bye, Melissa!

EXAMPLE 6.2. Solution.

ticipating students can certainly tell the teacher (and class) what they may say in this scenario while the teacher acts as the scribe.

7   The teacher may invite the whole class to work in pairs to come up with alternative solutions to the problem or think of new scenarios to act out. As the paired conversations occur, the teacher guides the students. Prompts such as "That solution is logical. It is likely that you can solve your problem in that way. What other solutions might be possible?"

Peer Collaboration and Extension

1   During this time, students work in heterogeneous groups. Students look around the room and collect several objects (e.g., crayons, books, scissors, markers).

2   Students work together to write their own scenario and script, including a problem and a solution, using their gathered objects. They should then practice for a performance. As they work, the teacher moves among the students, offering prompts and asking questions that support their performance such as, "Does the dialogue support the message the character wants to share? Think about the people in your audience. What details do they need to know?" During this time the teacher is also making note of the similar needs existing among the students. This information can help him or her to offer later interventions to students with similar needs.

3   Students role-play their scenarios with the class at a later time, such as in the following exchange:

> **Hamdi's little brother tore the pages in her library book. She is afraid to return the book because she may have to pay for it. What should she do?**
>
> MAX: Hey, Hamdi. What's that?
>
> HAMDI: My library book.
>
> SARAH: What's the matter?
>
> HAMDI: My little brother tore the pages, and now I'm afraid I'm going to have to pay for the book.
>
> MAX: Are you sure you will have to pay?
>
> HAMDI: I think so.
>
> SARAH: How about we tape the pages back together and tell the librarian what happened.
>
> HAMDI: Do you think that will be okay?
>
> MAX: I do! I have seen library books before that have been taped together. As long as we can read the words, I think it will be fine.
>
> HAMDI: Thanks, you two! I'll try it!

Teacher Differentiating and Accommodating

From the information the teacher gained as students worked collaboratively, he or she is now able to offer instruction that provides guided interventions to students with similar needs. As the teacher does so, the others read texts similar to those listed as suggested books, they can be engaged with the Tech It Out! activity or they can continue practicing their role-playing performances.

Beginning Level

Presenting a familiar object (e.g., a shoe), the teacher invites students to orally describe the object. Teachers can use a website to record the students' ideas. A name can be written next to each idea so students can "own" their contributions to the targeted word.

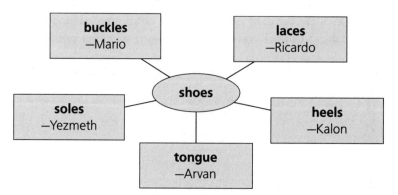

Intermediate Level: What Is It?

The teacher collects tangible objects or finds realistic pictures from the Internet. The students select one of these objects to describe. They describe the object orally, using the words *who, what, where, when,* and *why*. These target words can be written on 8″ × 11″ card stock and placed in the front of the classroom for easy reference. Students are encouraged to use these reference cards while speaking and writing. Students can bring in their own realia and be prepared to speak about the objects, or exchange objects with a partner.

> **TEACHER EXAMPLE**
>
> This is a bucket (*what*). My sister uses a bucket to build a sand castle (*who*). The bucket can hold water from the ocean (*where*). My sister loves to build sand castles on a hot summer day (*when*). The water from the bucket is used to add a moat to the sand castle (*why*).

Work Page 6.1 can be used with students as an organizational tool before they write their paragraphs.

Advanced Level: What Is This, What Is That?

Students select two objects that have been collected by the teacher and orally compare and contrast the objects using specific vocabulary that relates to the objects. The teacher records their vocabulary on a large chart for all to see. From the specific vocabulary related to the objects, the students create a folded graphic organizer to illustrate and support their descriptions (see Example 6.3).

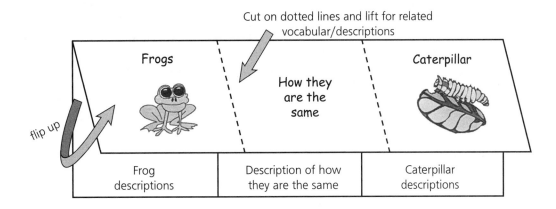

EXAMPLE 6.3. Folded graphic organizer.

Tech It Out!

The teacher videorecords a group of students orally describing or presenting an object/concept (e.g., lightning striking a tree). The video recording is played back for the class as partners guess what is being role-played or described. They could also discuss what made it easy or difficult to figure out the object or concept being described. The importance of detail in students' spoken vocabulary should be a priority during this activity. For ideas on video recording in the classroom, check out *www.idahoptv.org/learn/technology.cfm.*

Suggested Websites and Books

www.miguelmllop.com
www.alliance.brown.edu/tdl (Teaching Diverse Learners)
www.ncela.gwu.edu (National Clearinghouse for English Language Acquisition)

Ancona, George; Ada, Alma Flor; & Campoy, F. Isabel—*Mi Casa/My House* (2005); Children's Press.
Carle, Eric—*The Very Hungry Caterpillar* (2009); Philomel.
Herlong, M. H.—*The Great Wide Sea* (2010); Puffin.
Lewin, Ted—*Horse Song: The Naadam of Mongolia* (2008); Lee & Low Books.
Recorvits, Helen—*My Name Is Yoon* (2003); Farrar, Straus and Giroux.

References

Greenwood, S. C., & Flanigan, K. (2007). Overlapping vocabulary and comprehension: Context clues complement semantic gradients. *The Reading Teacher, 61*(3), 249–254.

Kornfeld, J., & Leyden, G. (2005). Acting out: Literature, drama, and connecting with history. *The Reading Teacher, 59*(3), 230–238.

Zehr, M. A. (2010). Tailoring lessons for English learners. *Education Week, 29*(19).

What Is It?

Name: _____

Objects I can use: _____   _____

_____   _____

_____   _____

_____   _____

Who	What	Where	When	Why

My Reading and Speaking Log

Common Core Standard

Determine the main idea of a text and explain how it is supported by key details; summarize the text

TESOL Standard

Discuss and summarize critical issues using visual or graphic support.

Focus skill: Comprehension
Secondary skill: Grammar

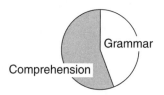

What Is the Purpose?

Use key details to summarize a text and orally share the summary.

What Is the Research Base?

Summarizing is a process of constructing meaning that involves receiving, comprehending, processing, and producing information (Ghazanfari & Sarani, 2009; McElvain, 2010; Moss & Young, 2010). Teaching students to move from the whole text to the essential elements of the text involves helping them strip away extraneous information to get to the essential information—the main idea and the key details. When students are able to summarize, they illustrate that they can solidify the information they have read and identify the salient information. *My Reading and Speaking Log* illustrates how to foster communication through shared response and careful monitoring.

Teacher Modeling and Guiding

1 The teacher begins by reading aloud a text, such as *Chato's Kitchen* by Gary Soto.

2 While reading, the teacher pauses after every couple of pages to model how he or she summarizes text. Using Work Page 7.1 helps students see how to record summary information.

3 Phrases may include "These first few pages were about . . . "; "As I think about the main idea, or the big idea in these pages, I know that. . . . "

4 The teacher continues this modeling throughout the text, adding new information to what was previously read. Phrases may include "Now, after reading a couple more pages, I can add to what I already know. Because I summarized by putting these main ideas together, I come up with. . . . "

5 When the students seem ready, they should be invited to offer suggestions that help the teacher summarize. As they do so, the teacher can also invite partner talk so that he or she can listen in to ensure that the students are understanding the information. The teacher might say to two students who are having trouble focusing on just the main idea, "You have many good ideas, but look at the picture and the words to see the one main idea. Notice how the cats are looking at the mice. What are their faces and the words telling us?"

6 Students' summary sentences of *Chato's Kitchen* are shown in Example 7.1.

Pages 1–2:	Chato hears five noisy mice.
Pages 3–4:	Chato invites the mice to dinner.
Pages 5–6:	The mice ask to bring a friend, Chorizo.
Pages 7–8:	Chato begins to prepare the dinner.
Pages 8–9:	Chato and his friend make tortillas.
Pages 10–11:	The cats are making a big dinner.
Pages 12–13:	The mice make quesadillas.
Pages 14–15:	Chorizo arrives and the mice go to Chato's house.
Page 16:	The cats are planning to eat the mice.
Page 17:	Chato sees that Chorizo is a dog.
Pages 18–19:	The cats hide from the dog.
Page 20:	The cats, mice, and dog eat together.

EXAMPLE 7.1. Students' Reading Summary Guide for *Chato's Kitchen*.

Peer Collaboration and Extension

1 During this time students work in heterogeneous groups.

2 After reading a shared text or the one read aloud by the teacher, students work to complete their own Reading Summary Guide (Work Page 7.1) together.

3 As they work, the teacher moves among the students, offering cues and prompts and asking questions that support their performance; for instance, "After reading a couple of pages you saw that several things happened. How can you put those ideas into one sentence? The three ideas you just mentioned can be combined to have one summary statement."

4 The teacher also makes note of the similar strengths and needs existing among the students. This information can help him or her to offer later interventions to students with similar needs.

5 While working, students take turns filling in the Reading Summary Guide, and all students are responsible for contributing to the content of what is recorded on the Work Page.

6 The teacher makes sure that all students are adding to the group's summary statements by asking them to initial their additions.

7 When finished, students orally practice sharing with the whole group.

8 While they are practicing, the teacher reminds the students to pay particular attention to the grammar and syntax of the language and to help each other with phrasing.

Teacher Differentiating and Accommodating

From the information the teacher gained as students worked collaboratively, he or she is now able to offer instruction that provides guided interventions to students with similar needs. As the teacher does so, the others can read texts similar to those listed as suggested books and completing a second Reading Summary Guide with a partner or practicing for their oral presentations. They can also be engaged in the Tech It Out! activity.

Beginning Level

The teacher writes a message on the board or on a large chart, giving deliberate miscues in one specific area of grammar (e.g., plurals = *foots*, past tense = *I go yesterday*). Together the students read the message aloud as a shared reading and correct the message as an entire group or class. The teacher then summarizes the main idea illustrated by the combination of sentences. (We enjoyed a day at the zoo.)

EXAMPLE: Focus—Past Tense

Daily Message, October 17

I was so happy to see you today. Yesterday we going to the zoo and seeing a lot of animals. The bears was asleep in their caves and the tigers eated.

Intermediate Level

In advance, the teacher prepares copies of a "Daily Message" for each student. The Daily Message may be "toda iz the first da fo spreeng." The message is also displayed on a document camera or on a large chart for all to see. Each student works with a partner as they read the message and orally discuss the syntactic, semantic, and morphophonemic miscues. Students record their corrections on their copies of the Daily Message. The entire class regroups, and the teacher and students record the corrections on the message that is displayed on the document camera or large chart. The activity concludes with the teacher and students working together to write a summary statement related to the shared information. If the students hesitate to participate, the teacher returns again to a text and models how to develop a summary statement.

Advanced Level

At the close of a unit on a specific area of grammar instruction (e.g., noun–verb agreement), students work in small groups or as partners, writing their own Daily Messages with deliberate syntactic, semantic, and morphophonemic miscues. Students write ungrammatical messages trying to fool the other students. Students exchange their messages with partners or another group and record their corrections on the messages. Students justify their corrections by stating the grammar rule or by giving an appropriate example. They then make a summary statement related to the message intent.

Tech It Out!

Using PowerPoint, Apple's Keynote, or other presentation software, the teacher or students can create a slide show, summarizing the theme and supporting details of what they are reading. After the user chooses a theme, the software provides him or her an opportunity to add text, graphics, and even media with personally developed words and images. Each slide can relate to a specific part of the theme or to a character's traits as portrayed in the story. As a concluding activity after reading a book, the first slide might give the overall theme and information regarding the setting; the second slide may present information about a specific trait a character exhibits; the third slide may present three or four examples of how and where the trait is exemplified. More limited approaches may narrow the process to a demonstration of one specific detail as related to a character's trait that students develop as they read. They could then engage in discussions related to the traits and the supporting evidence they identify in a text. Students can have fun designing each slide and adding sound effects, animation, media clips and artful graphics, or their own creative designs. For ideas on using PowerPoint in the classroom, check out *www.internet4classrooms.com/ideas_pp.htm*. Students may also enjoy sharing their thinking through a Glog. Check out *http://kpercle.edu.glogster.com/creating-a-glog/*.

Suggested Websites and Books

www.meade.k12.sd.us/PASS
www.readingrockets.org/strategies/summarizing
www.languagearts.pppst.com/summarize.html

Awdry, Rev. W.—*Thomas' ABC Book* (1998); Random House Books for Young Readers.
Coy, John—*Around the World* (2005); Lee & Low Books.
Katz, Karen—*My First Chinese New Year* (2004); Henry Holt.
Kurtz, Jane—*In the Small Small Night* (2005); Greenwillow Books.
Thomas, Joyce Carol—*Linda Brown, You Are Not Alone* (2003); Hyperion Books.

References

Ghazanfari, M., & Sarani, A. (2009). The wonder of reading: The effect of generative study strategies on EFL learners' reading comprehension and recall of short stories. *Indian Journal of Applied Linguistics*, 35(2), 87–100.

McElvain, C. M. (2010). Transactional literature circles and the reading comprehension of English learners in the mainstream classroom. *Journal of Research in Reading*, 33(2), 178–205.

Moss, B., & Young, T. A. (2010). *Creating lifelong readers through independent reading*. Newark, DE: International Reading Association.

Reading Summary Guide

Name: _____ Story/Chapter Title: _____ Date: _____

Page/ Paragraph	Summary Statement
	1. _____
	_____
	_____
	2. _____
	_____
	_____
	3. _____
	_____
	_____
	4. _____
	_____
	_____
	5. _____
	_____
	_____
	6. _____
	_____
	_____
	7. _____
	_____
	_____
	8. _____
	_____
	_____

Writing for Different Purposes

Focus skill: Comprehension
Secondary skill: Vocabulary

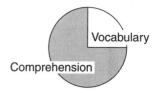

What Is the Purpose?

Understand perspective and purpose when writing.

What Is the Research Base?

Research suggests that reading and writing activities promote students' control of grammatical, syntactic, semantic, and spoken aspects of language (Cloud, Lakin, Leininger, & Maxwell, 2010; Cullen, 2003; Simon, 2008). *Writing for Different Purposes* is based on a strategy called RAFT, developed by Holston and Santa (1985), through which students collaborate to develop a written scenario that communicates a specific message to an intended audience. After an oral presentation of their scenarios by various groups, the class tries to guess the intended role, audience, format, and topic each group endeavored to portray.

Teacher Modeling and Guiding

1 The teacher begins this lesson by explaining how authors write for different purposes (see Example 8.1).

2 The term *RAFT* is then explained and charted for all to see: R = Role; A = Audience; F = Format; T = Topic.

3 Next the teacher shows students the read-aloud for this lesson and identifies the role, audience, format, and topic prior to reading so students know what to focus on while listening. *A Bad Case of Stripes* by David Shannon would work well here.

4 After the read-aloud, the teacher models his or her thinking about the role, audience, format, and topic. For example: "I know that because my purpose for writing today is to share a friendly letter, I need to think of the greeting, body, and closing of the letter. I also need to think about who is doing the writing. In the case of our story today, I am doing the writing but I will be thinking like our main character (Camilla Cream) mother and my writing voice will come from the perspective or thinking of the main character's mother. I need to really think about how the mother would feel and how she would act as I write this letter. Help me with this." Together the teacher and students create the lesson using the RAFT format.

Role: Marine biologists **A**udience: Sea World employees **F**ormat: Conference speakers **T**opic: The feeding habits of penguins

Group 1

Role: Whale trainer **A**udience: Whale show audience **F**ormat: Informative speech **T**opic: The differences between types of whales

Group 2

Rrole: Radio commercial singers **A**udience: Radio listeners **F**ormat: A song sung to the tune of "Row, Row, Row Your Boat" **T**opic: The migration patterns of gray whales

Group 3

Role: A pod of dolphins **A**udience: One another **F**ormat: A conversation **T**opic: Organizing fish hunts

Group 4

Rrole: Television actors **A**udience: Television audience **F**ormat: Public service commercial **T**opic: The effects of contaminants on our beaches and the importance of keeping beaches clean

Group 5

Role: Interviewer and professors **A**udience: Television audience **F**ormat: Interview (local news program) **T**opic: The feeding and social practices of humpback whales

Group 6

EXAMPLE 8.1. RAFT examples.

R: Camilla's mother
A: Doctors
F: Friendly letter
T: Please help my daughter get well

Peer Collaboration and Extension

1 During this time, students work in heterogeneous groups.

2 Prior to this group work, the teacher has written many different RAFTs on strips of paper and placed these in a paper bag.

3 A student in each group reaches inside the paper bag to select a RAFT. Only the R, A, F, and T cues are listed. Reaching inside the bag, the student grabs a slip of paper that says, for example:

R = Bob
A = His mother
F = E-mail
T = Send food

4 Each RAFT is read aloud by a group member, and the students work together to create related appropriate text. Using Work Page 8.1 can help with this task.

5 The teacher assigns students to heterogeneous groups and, as they work, moves among them offering cues and prompts and asking questions that support their performance. For example, if students do not have enough information about how to feed whales or penguins, the teacher may have available books like *The Whale Family Book* by Cynthia d'Vincent or invite them to watch videos such as *www.youtube. com/watch?v=LR9L_k_GJEo*. As the students work, the teacher makes note of the similar needs existing among them. This information will help him or her to offer later interventions to students with similar needs.

6 A RAFT can also be drawn if students are not yet able to write one. After all groups have met and developed their RAFTs, a whole-class discussion can occur in which similarities and differences are shared about perspective and writing purposes. If time is limited, a group can share with just one other. This sharing supports the idea of writing for an audience and promotes oral language.

7 Based on students' developing proficiencies, groups of students can now read a shared text (perhaps from their reading anthology or a *Weekly Reader* or other magazine) and create their own RAFTs. A RAFT can be completed by the group creating it, or the creating group can ask another group to complete it.

Teacher Differentiating and Accommodating

From the information the teacher gained as students worked collaboratively, he or she is now able to offer instruction that provides guided interventions to students with similar needs. As the teacher does so, the others can read texts similar to those listed as suggested books, and create challenge RAFTs, or be engaged with the Tech It Out! activity.

Beginning Level

This strategy enables teachers to model their thought processes as they prepare to write. The teacher "talks" while jotting down ideas about how an author gets ideas for writing and the process that moves these ideas into a written text. The students listen as the teacher models. After the teacher models thinking aloud about writing, pairs of students think aloud about the same topic or text that was presented by the teacher. When finished, students share their thinking. This oral rehearsal can help students before they write independently.

> **EXAMPLE**
>
> The following write-aloud was done after reading the text *What's under the Sea?* The teacher modeled her thinking as she focused on the characters, settings, problem, and solution.

"Yesterday we read the book *What's under the Sea?* Remember how we loved the idea of reading about the animals that live in the ocean and some of the problems they have with food and their enemies? As I was reading the book to you, I thought, *Wouldn't it be GREAT to write a book like it, but use different characters, setting, problems, and solutions?* For example, I was thinking, as an author, if I wrote a story about what's under my shoe, the readers can read about small insects that live on the ground and the problems they have with food and their enemies. I like the idea of "under my shoe," so I already have a setting. As I think through my story and create my characters, I can also think about the problems they may have. We have studied about all kinds of insects so I know a lot about them. My characters will probably be insects.

"I think I will call my story 'What's under My Shoe?' I will start the story with my character, Annabelle Ant, who lives on the ground outside my house. I think that maybe her problem can be that she is afraid of the bigger flying insects that are taking her food. I already have my characters, my setting, and a problem. (The teacher may need to review each.) I know that I can think of a solution as I write. I think that I am ready to write."

Intermediate Level

Using various writing prompts, the students practice writing for different purposes. The teacher interactively models how to create an example of the target genre being written (e.g., RAFT, poem, story, report, dialogue, letter). This RAFT example is charted on large chart paper. When the modeling is complete, a situational scenario is shared with students. Together the teacher and students generate specific vocabulary related to the scenario, and the students' language is recorded by the teacher on the board or chart paper for the students to use. Oral language is developed as students work in pairs or small groups to create an oral draft of their text and think about the written draft. Students can exchange writing samples with other students at the end of the lesson.

SITUATIONAL SCENARIO EXAMPLE

You would like to invite the principal to a birthday party. Write an invitation to the principal and present it to the class. The RAFT for this activity can be *R* = students; *A* = principal; *F* = invitation; *T* = Come to my party.

Advanced Level

Students create wanted posters for famous and infamous characters in literature. The posters should tell who is wanted, why the person is wanted, his or her physical attributes/description, and what the reward might be. Students can create wanted posters for real-life musicians, television or media stars, or personalities as well. Students should be reminded to be respectful in their descriptions. These can be shared with partners, in small groups, or with the whole class.

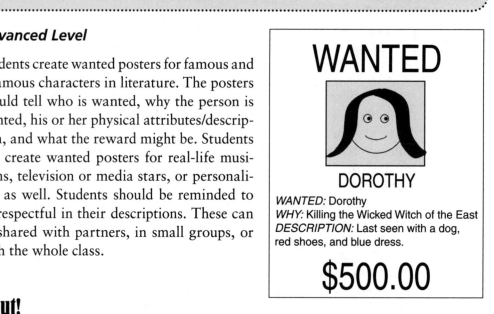

WANTED

DOROTHY

WANTED: Dorothy
WHY: Killing the Wicked Witch of the East
DESCRIPTION: Last seen with a dog, red shoes, and blue dress.

$500.00

Tech It Out!

Students can search websites such as *www.teachingheart.net/readerstheater.htm* or *www.aaronshep.com/rt/RTE.html* for Reader's Theatre scripts or write their own using Microsoft Word or other word processing programs. The teacher or a student "director" can videotape the group, using a camcorder. Student-prepared costumes, realia, and backdrops can add to the fun of the performance. DVDs or movies can be made of the productions and shared with parents on Parents Night or with other classes at the school. For a list of great Reader's Theatre scripts, try *www.teaching-*

heart.net/readerstheater.htm or *www.readingonline.org.* Once at the website, go to "Search." Enter the words "Reader's Theatre Scripts." Scripts can also support students as they develop ideas for their writing and performance of additional RAFTs.

Suggested Websites and Books

www.writingfix.com/wac/RAFT.htm
www.readingquest.org
www.learnnc.org/lp/pages/672
www2.scholastic.com/browse/collection.jsp?id=233.

Bruchac, Joseph—*Our Stories Remember: American Indian History, Culture, and Values through Storytelling* (2003); Fulcrum Publishing.
Fox, Mem—*Whoever You Are* (2006); Sandpiper.
Hoffman, Mary—*The Color of Home* (2002); Dial.
Mandelbaum, Pili—*You Be Me, I'll Be You* (1990); Kane/Miller Books.
McDonald, Megan—*My House Has Stars* (2001); Scholastic.

References

Cloud, N., Lakin, J., Leininger, E., & Maxwell, L. (2010). *Teaching adolescent English language learners: Essential strategies for middle and high school.* Philadelphia: Caslon Publishing.

Cullen, R. (2003). *6+ traits of writing.* New York: Scholastic.

Holston, V., & Santa, C. (1985). RAFT: A method of writing across the curriculum that works. *Journal of Reading, 28*(5), 456–457.

Simon, L. (2008). I wouldn't choose it, but I don't regret reading it: Scaffolding students' engagement with complex texts. *Journal of Adolescent and Adult Literacy, 52*(2), 134–143.

Writing for Different Purposes

Name: _____

Role: **A**udience: **F**ormat: **T**opic: **Group 1**	**R**ole: **A**udience: **F**ormat: **T**opic: **Group 2**
Role: **A**udience: **F**ormat: **T**opic: **Group 3**	**R**ole: **A**udience: **F**ormat: **T**opic: **Group 4**
Role: **A**udience: **F**ormat: **T**opic: **Group 5**	**R**ole: **A**udience: **F**ormat: **T**opic: **Group 6**

Total Physical Response with Pictures

Common Core Standard

Identify real-life connections between words and their use.

TESOL Standard

Role-play situations in small groups based on dialogues, video clips, or field trips.

Focus skill: Vocabulary
Secondary skill: Comprehension

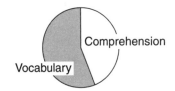

What Is the Purpose?

Match vocabulary words with images.

What Is the Research Base?

Total Physical Response with Pictures is based on the premise that listening is an information-gathering activity that involves visualizing, predicting, and using prior knowledge to comprehend and confirm shared information. Listening and speaking activities provide opportunities for students to focus on word meanings as a pathway to comprehension and vocabulary development (Chun, 2009; Mordaunt & Olson, 2010; Pappamihiel & Mihai, 2006). *Total Physical Response with Pictures* benefits both listeners and speakers as language is generated, organized, and interpreted. The activity is designed to provide a format for students to hear and interpret words they hear as their teacher and classmates describe words and concepts from trade texts, textbooks, or magazines.

Teacher Modeling and Guiding

1 Prior to reading a poem about snowmen, the teacher displays a picture of a snowman (see Example 9.1). For poems about snowmen, see *http://www.hellum. com/items/1257042-snowmen*.

2 Before reading the poem aloud, the teacher draws a picture of a snowman and then labels parts of the snowman, using Work Page 9.1 (i.e., hat, nose, arms, mouth), and invites students to say the word for each part of the snowman.

3 The teacher encourages the students to repeat the words and point to each object on their own bodies.

4 As the teacher reads the poem, the students are invited to chime in when they feel confident and to point to their body parts simultaneously.

5 The teacher stops periodically and models how to think about these words. "I see the word *hat* in my poem. I know that a *hat* is worn on my head [points to his or her head] and that it keeps me warm if it is cold outside and shades my face when it is hot and sunny. Hats can be used for many different things."

6 The poem (or other text) should be read several times, encouraging more and more students to read along and use physical responses to learn vocabulary words.

Peer Collaboration and Extension

1 During this time students work in heterogeneous groups. On a large piece of chart paper, or using Work Page 9.1, students sketch an object.

2 Students take turns labeling the parts of the object.

3 As they work, the teacher moves among the students, offering cues and prompts and asking questions that support their performance. If they are unable to think of a label for part of the object, the teacher may tell them; if they have heard it before, the teacher may prompt the students with a question that reminds them. For example, he or she might say, " I see that you have drawn your picture of a tree.

EXAMPLE 9.1. Snowman picture.

Now can you add a word that tells who lives in a tree? Whose habitat is a tree?" The teacher also makes note of the similar needs existing among the students. This information can help him or her to offer later interventions to students with similar needs.

4 If time permits, students can show their labeled sketches, noting the vocabulary words written as labels on the image.

Teacher Differentiating and Accommodating

From the information the teacher gained as students worked collaboratively, he or she is now able to offer instruction that provides guided interventions to students with similar needs. As the teacher does so, the others can be reading and listening to texts on tape similar to those listed as suggested books, they can be engaged with the Tech It Out! activity, or they can continue creating pictures and adding supportive language. They may also be drawing and labeling additional objects or pictures related to a book they have just listened to or read.

Beginning Level

After selecting and charting particularly tricky vocabulary or concepts for students, the teacher reads these while modeling possible movements. Students repeat words and mimic these movements. Together, the teacher and students talk about the movements, again saying the words that accompany particular movements.

> **EXAMPLE: Book for Beginning Level—*Deep in the Forest***
>
> After reading aloud *Deep in the Forest*, the teacher helps the students create movements that "show" the bear in the story (e.g., arms raised with fingers like claws, mouth open as if roaring). The teacher models each action, with the students mimicking. Once the movements are established and students have talked about each movement and word, they act out the story as the teacher reads aloud. Possible movements for *Deep in the Forest* include:
>
> Tiptoeing inside
> Eating porridge
> Sitting in chairs
> Sleeping in beds
> Running away

> **EXAMPLE: Song for Beginning Level—*"Mrs. Gooney Bird"***
>
> Favorite class songs can be matched to movements in the same way. The teacher creates specific movements that connect with the words in the song, modeling the movements as the song is sung with the class. Possible movements for "Mrs. Gooney Bird" include:
>
> Right arm, left arm
> Right foot, left foot
> Peck away, turn around

Intermediate/Advanced Level

Using a text at the intermediate/advanced level, such as a poem from Shel Silverstein or Jack Prelutsky, students create charts illustrating words and related movements. Students work individually, with partners, or in small groups. When finished, students teach the class their words and innovative movements as they invite peer participation. These activities give students multiple opportunities to practice their oral language skills while teaching their peers the movements that accompany selected words and phrases. A chart can also be developed and labeled with numbers. Number cards are passed out to the students, and when the particular part of the poem is read aloud the student holding the corresponding number card acts out the movement.

Tech It Out!

Students work in pairs to conduct a search for images, using Google or some other search engine. For example, student 1 displays, on the computer screen, an image of a girl bouncing a basketball while student 2 gets in the same position shown in the image. By doing so, student 2 brings the image to life. Students then use the word or concept illustrated by the image in a sentence or story. These sentences or stories should add life to the images. The teacher offers examples of how to make these images come to life in a sentence or story. For example, if the image is a cat playing with a ball of yarn next to a young girl, the related sentence could be *A fluffy cat would be a perfect pet.* A sentence for an image of green grass could be *I love the smell of freshly cut green grass.* For additional images, students can try *www. nationalgeographic.com/kids.*

Suggested Websites and Books

www.tprsource.com/asher.htm

www.eslresources.wordpress.com/category/eslefl-resources/activity-type/total-physical-response

www.colorincolorado.org/educators/content/oral

Johnson, Angela—*Just Like Josh Gibson* (2007); Simon & Schuster Children's Publishing.

Laden, Nina—*Peek-A-Who?* (2000); Chronicle Books.

Li, Shuyuan; Chau, Aaron; & Wei, Deborah—*Walking on Solid Ground* (Aesop) Accolades (Awards) (2004); Philadelphia Folklore Project.

Rockwell, Thomas—*How to Eat Fried Worms* (2006); Yearling.

San Souci, Robert D.—*Cut from the Same Cloth: American Women of Myth, Legend and Tall Tale* (2000); Putnam Juvenile.

References

Chun, C. W. (2009). Critical literacies and graphic novels for English-language learners: Teaching *Maus. Journal of Adolescent and Adult Literacy, 53*(2), 144–153.

Mordaunt, O., & Olson, D. (2010). Listen, listen, listen and listen: Building a comprehension corpus and making it comprehensible. *Educational Studies, 36*(3), 249–258.

Pappamihiel, N. E., & Mihai, F. (2006). Assessing English language learners' content knowledge in middle school classrooms. *Middle School Journal, 38*(1), 34–43.

What I Draw, I Can Label

Name: _____

I can put labels on my picture.

Expanding Word Knowledge

Common Core Standard

Determine or clarify the meaning of unknown and multiple-meaning words and phrases based on context.

TESOL Standard

Identify targeted vocabulary nonverbally (e.g., pointing out cognates) during guided reading of visually supported multicultural text.

Focus skill: Vocabulary
Secondary skill: Pronunciation

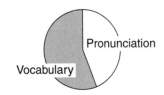

What Is the Purpose?

Visualize, predict, and comprehend vocabulary in context.

What Is the Research Base?

Vocabulary knowledge enhances reading comprehension (Graves, 2005; Lervag & Aukrust, 2010). *Expanding Word Knowledge* provides students an opportunity to relate information gained from visualizing, predicting, and making personal connections with the meaning and spelling of content-area vocabulary (Farstrup & Samuels, 2008). Through this activity, teachers can share real-world as well as academic language knowledge with their students.

Teacher Modeling and Guiding

1 The teacher begins this lesson by talking about how words can sometimes have different meanings depending on the context.

2 For instance, the teacher thinks aloud about the word *target* and explains that it has more than one meaning and that we have to think about the sentence in which it appears to know which definition is being used. The teacher and the students discuss the idea that *target* can mean something we aim for in archery or when playing darts and that it is also a word used to identify a focus, as in *target words*.

3 To illustrate the idea of expanding word knowledge, the teacher reads aloud a text about brush fires. For examples visit *topics.nytimes.com/top/news/science/topics/forest_and_brush_fires/index.html*.

4 As the teacher reads, he or she models how to think about the word *brush* and pauses to fill in Work Page 10.1. At first, the teacher may talk about a brush as an object used to brush hair. Next the teacher can model how to think about alternative definitions for the word *brush*. "I am going to read an article about brush fires. I know what *fire* means, but I wonder why anyone would have a fire in a hairbrush. Wouldn't a person's hair catch on fire? I bet the author is talking about another kind of brush fire. Let's see, if I keep reading I learn that brush fires happen a lot where there is dry land. As I look at this picture here and these words, the article says that there are a lot of brush fires in California. Now I am learning that there are other definitions of *brush*. I am realizing that a brush fire doesn't have anything to do with my hair. It has to do with the environment and the dry land. That sure would make more sense. Good thing the author and illustrator gave me so many picture and word clues." Articles about brush fires can be found at *http://topics.nytimes.com/top/news/science/topics/forest_and_brush_fires/index.html*.

5 As the teacher models this thinking of multiple meanings, the following expanded word knowledge chart is developed:

EXPANDED WORD KNOWLEDGE

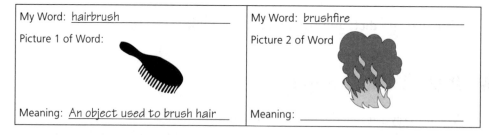

My Word: <u>hairbrush</u>

Picture 1 of Word:

Meaning: <u>An object used to brush hair</u>

My Word: <u>brushfire</u>

Picture 2 of Word

Meaning: _____

Peer Collaboration and Extension

1 Prior to introducing this lesson the teacher prepares a set of multiple meaning word cards with pictures, written on 3″ × 5″ cards (or students make their own sets, using words such as *set* and *set*, *game* and *game*).

2 Cards are placed face down, and students must find two words that make a match. Once students find two words that are the same, they must contextualize the words.

3 During this time students work in heterogeneous groups. As they work, the teacher moves among the students, offering cues and prompts and asking questions that support their performance. For example, the teacher might say, "That's one example of the word *trip*, now let's think about another way you could use this word to tell when you are taking a vacation with your family." The teacher also makes note of the similar needs existing among the students. This information will help him or her to offer later interventions to students with similar needs.

The following are examples of what two students said as evidence of their understanding of *bat* and *book*.

> JAIME: I found *bat* here and *bat* there. [Holds up cards.] I know that a bat can be used to hit a ball. A bat is also a flying animal.
>
> SAYED: I found *book* over here and *book* right there. One book is what you read and the other book is what happens when someone makes a time to meet you. When my Mom says that she has booked a date with my grandmother, then she writes the meeting time on the calendar.

Teacher Differentiating and Accommodating

From the information the teacher gained as students worked collaboratively, he or she is now able to offer instruction that provides guided interventions to students with similar needs. As the teacher does so, the others can read texts similar to those listed as suggested books or create additional word cards to add to the vocabulary game. They may also be engaged with the Tech It Out! activity.

Beginning Level

The teacher and the students brainstorm a list of homographs (words that are pronounced and spelled the same but have different meanings). The teacher can use

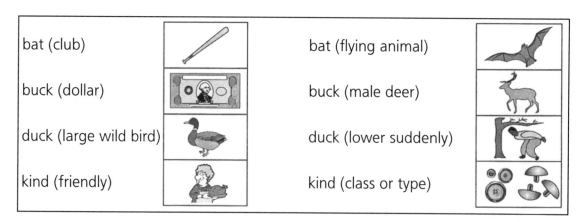

EXAMPLE 10.1. Homograph examples.

Fry and Kress's *The Reading Teacher's Book of Lists, 6th Edition* (Jossey-Bass, 2006) or *www.all-about-spelling.com/list-of-homophones.html* for a list of homographs. Words are charted on a large piece of paper with illustrations for support (see Example 10.1). The teacher pronounces each word, encouraging students to echo the pronunciation. Students use the words in sentences, class discussion, partner conversations, and during independent writing time.

Intermediate Level

The teacher and the students brainstorm a list of homophones (words that sound the same but are spelled differently and have different meanings) as they interactively create a large chart. The teacher can use Fry and Kress's *The Reading Teacher's Book of Lists, 6th Edition* (Jossey-Bass, 2006) or *www.educationoasis.com/curriculum/Lang_Arts/resources/homophones.htm* for a list of homophones (see also Example 10.2). As words are added to the class chart, the teacher models the pronunciation and the students echo-read each word. In order to comprehend the meaning of each set of words, pairs of students use the words in sentences, in conversations, and in their written work.

Advanced Level

The teacher and students work together, discussing the synonyms for words that are commonly used in the class. This is a perfect time to introduce students to a thesaurus. The teacher discusses how knowing these synonyms helps us to use precise language. The teacher may use paint chips (from a local paint store) in hues of the same color to help students understand shades of meaning. In this way, students discover how many different words can be used for a meaning by writing a string of synonyms. Students can orally present their synonym strings to the class.

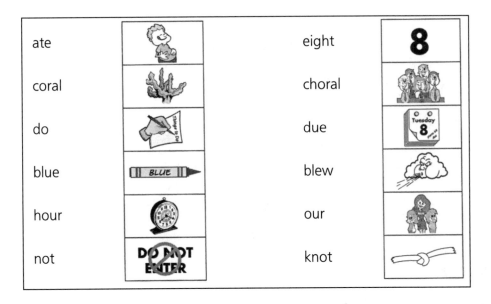

EXAMPLE 10.2. Homophone examples.

EXAMPLE: *happy–pleased–delighted–overjoyed*
(may be shown by Hues/Shades of Blue)

happy	pleased	delighted	overjoyed

Tech It Out!

In pairs, students can expand their vocabulary by substituting target words with synonyms. These word banks can be created by students using Microsoft Word or other word processing programs. Student 1 may write a sentence using a different-colored font for the target word. Student 2 can use the thesaurus (under the "Tools" heading) and rewrite the sentence using a synonym for the target word. Student 1 can switch roles with Student 2 as they discuss the meanings of words and whether or not a particular word suggested by the thesaurus makes sense in the sentence. As students work together, they can keep a word bank of newly acquired vocabulary. For lists of words and additional ideas about studying words, visit *english.donnay-oung.org/words.htm*.

Suggested Websites and Books

www.eastoftheweb.com/games
www.funbrain.com/kidscenter.html
www.learninggamesforkids.com/word_games.html

Boynton, Sandra—*Blue Hat, Green Hat* (1984); Little Simon.
Freedman, Russell—*Lincoln: A Photobiography* (1989); Sandpiper.
O'Dell, Scott—*Island of the Blue Dolphins* (2010); Sandpiper.
Silverstein, Shel—*Where the Sidewalk Ends: Poems and Drawings* (1974).
Taylor, Mildred—*Roll of Thunder, Hear My Cry* (2004); Puffin.

References

Farstrup, A. E., & Samuels, S. J. (Eds.) (2008). *What research has to say about vocabulary instruction*. Newark, DE: International Reading Association.

Graves, M. (2005). *Vocabulary book*. Newark, DE: International Reading Association.

Lervag, A., & Aukrust, V. G. (2010). Vocabulary knowledge is a critical determinant of the difference in reading comprehension growth between first and second language learners. *Journal of Child Psychology and Psychiatry, 51*(5), 612–620.

Expanded Word Knowledge

My Word: _____	My Word: _____
Picture 1 of Word:	Picture 2 of Word
Meaning: _____	Meaning: _____
My Word: _____	My Word: _____
Picture 1 of Word:	Picture 2 of Word
Meaning: _____	Meaning: _____
My Word: _____	My Word: _____
Picture 1 of Word:	Picture 2 of Word
Meaning: _____	Meaning: _____
My Word: _____	My Word: _____
Picture 1 of Word:	Picture 2 of Word
Meaning: _____	Meaning: _____
My Word: _____	My Word: _____
Picture 1 of Word:	Picture 2 of Word
Meaning: _____	Meaning: _____

My Read-Aloud Listening/Discussion Guide

Common Core Standard

Determine the main idea of a text, recounting the key details and explaining how they support the theme, plot, or essential information.

TESOL Standard

Discuss and summarize text-related issues using visual or graphic support.

Focus skill: Comprehension
Secondary skill: Pronunciation

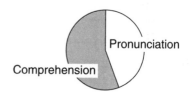

What Is the Purpose?

Anticipate, visualize, and connect new information with prior knowledge as a way to support understanding of texts heard and read.

What Is the Research Base?

Reading comprehension is a result of multifaceted skills, including vocabulary knowledge, decoding skills, general cognitive ability, and interpretation (Goldenberg & Coleman, 2010; Ketch, 2005; Laufer & Ravenhorst-Kalvoski, 2010). *My Read-Aloud Listening/Discussion Guide* provides teachers a means to model and promote an integrated skills approach when introducing new linguistic structures and vocabulary words that may be derived from narrative stories.

Teacher Modeling and Guiding

1 As the teacher reads a text aloud, he or she models how to think about what is being read.

2 The teacher must be explicit as he or she talks about how readers *anticipate* what they will read, picture *images* in their minds, and *connect* new information with what they already know in order to *understand* the text.

3 As the teacher reads, he or she pauses to fill in Work Page 11.1 to let students in on his or her thinking and make the reading processes transparent to students.

4 For example, a teacher who is reading about the earth's outside layer of crust may say, "I see that the title says 'The Earth's Crust'. I know that has something to do with layers and how parts of the earth are hotter than others. Let me fill in this first section with what I think this passage is going to be about." The teacher models for students how to fill in 1, 2, and 3 on the Read-Aloud Listening/Discussion Guide.

5 The teacher continues with this process of reading, pausing to fill in the Work Page, and returning to his or her reading.

6 During the lesson, the teacher is continuously showing students explicitly how readers go from anticipating information, to visualizing more information, connecting new information with prior knowledge, and finally coming to an understanding of the new information.

7 This idea of listening to what is read and pausing to discuss and record information is essential to students' listening comprehension during a read-aloud.

Peer Collaboration and Extension

1 During this time, students work in heterogeneous groups. Students assume different roles: reader, anticpator, visualizer, connector, understander.

2 One student reads a passage or book and other students take turns fulfilling their roles.

3 As they work the teacher moves among the students, offering cues and prompts and asking questions that support their performance. The teacher may say, "As the anticipator, your job is to predict what you are about to read. You can look to clues on this page to help with your job of predicting."

4 The teacher also makes note of the similar needs existing among the students. This information can help him or her to offer later interventions to students with similar needs.

5 It is important to note that students may contribute to the discussion out of order, inasmuch as good readers anticipate, visualize, connect, and come to an understanding about text at different times.

6 Working as a group, students fill out a Read-Aloud Listening/Discussion Guide as a group to document their thinking as they read and listen to the target text.

Teacher Differentiating and Accommodating

From the information the teacher gained as students worked collaboratively, he or she is now able to offer instruction that provides guided interventions to students with similar needs. As the teacher does so, the others can read texts similar to those listed as suggested books or can complete their Read-Aloud Listening/Discussion Guide. They may also be engaged with the Tech It Out! activity.

Beginning Level

While sharing a page from a big book such as *Jasper's Bean-stalk* (Butterworth & Inkpen, 1997), the teacher asks students to name specific items they see. The teacher records these items as vocabulary words on sticky notes and places them on the picture. After vocabulary is generated, the teacher asks the students to each turn to a partner and, using the generated vocabulary, predict what the story may be about. The  teacher records students' predictions on chart paper or sentence strips. As the text is read, the teacher stops at selected sections to confirm predictions, discussing with the class members why their predictions were correct and what elements in the text supported their predictions.

Intermediate Level

During a read-aloud, the teacher stops periodically so students can have a conversation with their peers about what they understand about the story elements of the text. After the teacher reads the text aloud, students, in small groups or as partners, use a graphic organizer to list the characters, setting, problem, and solution from a given text (see Example 11.1). As the teacher reads the text

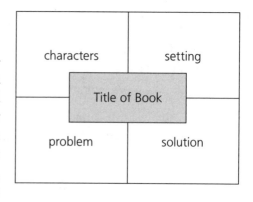

characters	setting
	Title of Book	
problem	solution

EXAMPLE 11.1. Graphic organizer.

aloud, students record ideas and key vocabulary words that relate to the text. They illustrate their work and/or write one or two sentences for each section. As a concluding activity, students share their ideas with another partner, a small group, or the whole class.

Advanced Level

As the teacher reads a text aloud, students make text-to-self, text-to-text, and text-to-world connections. Students record their connections on sticky notes. At the conclusion of the read-aloud the students place the sticky notes on a chart similar to the one shown in Example 11.2. The students have a whole-class discussion as connections are shared and sticky notes are manipulated among the columns. Students' oral language is developed as they "defend" why they placed a sticky note in a particular column.

Tech It Out!

Using Microsoft Excel spreadsheets, students create their own graphic organizers as note-taking guides during a read-aloud lesson. On their charts, students can record their predictions, connections, and/or questions to the author. Students are encouraged to tell about the different ways of organizing their thoughts during a small- or whole-group sharing/discussion time. By using Excel, some students may want to take the information from the spreadsheet and create pie charts and/or graphs about how often they are making connections, predicting, or questioning the author. Students can share their strategies with one another in small- and whole-group settings. Any technology wizards in the class can also demonstrate their graphic organizers and their usefulness in a PowerPoint presentation. For ideas about using Excel in a variety of ways in the classroom, visit *learntech.ties.k12.mn.us/Excel_Classroom_Projects*.

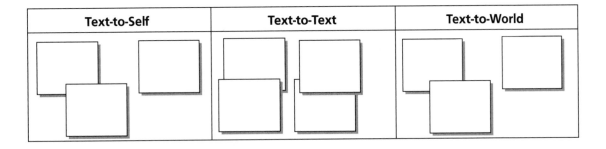

EXAMPLE 11.2. Sticky-notes chart.

> ### Suggested Websites and Books
>
> *www.proteacher.com/070001.shtml*
> *www.teachervision.fen.com/reading/resource/48646.html*
> *www.readaloudamerica.org*
>
> Ada, Alma Flor—*I Love Saturdays y Domingos* (2004); Atheneum.
> MacLachlan, Patricia—*Sarah Plain and Tall* (2004); HarperCollins.
> Steptoe, John—*Mufaro's Beautiful Daughters: An African Tale* (1993); HarperFestival.
> Twain, Mark—*The Adventures of Tom Sawyer* (2009); NewSouth.
> Weeks, Sarah—*Splish, Splash!* (2000); HarperCollins.

References

Goldenberg, C., & Coleman, R. (2010). *Promoting academic achievement among English learners: A guide to the research.* Thousand Oaks, CA: Corwin Press.

Ketch, A. (2005). Conversation: The comprehension connection. *The Reading Teacher, 59,* 8–13.

Laufer, B., & Ravenhorst-Kalvoski, G. C. (2010). Lexical threshold revisited: Lexical text coverage, learners' vocabulary size and reading comprehension. *Reading in a Foreign Language, 22*(1), 15–30.

Read-Aloud Listening/Discussion Guide

Name: _____

1. The context of what I hear will be (e.g., a narrative text, an informational text, a song, or a poem):

_____

2. The title is: _____

3. I anticipate hearing about (e.g., content, main ideas, themes, problems): _____

_____

4. This is a picture that comes to my mind when I hear the word (e.g., theme, vocabulary word, or main concept):

_____

_____

_____

_____

Illustration Box

5. My knowledge about this topic is helped because of my familiarity with: _____

_____

_____

6. As I listen, I understand: _____

_____

_____

_____

Pause 1: Discuss answers with a partner. Share ideas and summarize text so far. _____

_____

_____

_____

Pause 2: Discuss, share, and summarize text up to this point. _____

_____

_____

New words I am learning:

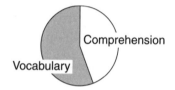

Strategy Lesson 12

Word Maps

Focus skill: Vocabulary
Secondary skill: Comprehension

Common Core Standard

Analyze the structure an author uses to organize a text, including how the major sections and language contribute to the whole and to the development of the ideas.

TESOL Standard

Contribute vocabulary or match to illustrated word charts, games, or other materials with a partner to support comprehension.

What Is the Purpose?

Utilize word and concept maps to support understanding of vocabulary and concepts.

What Is the Research Base?

Research suggests that vocabulary can be expanded by associating new and familiar words and concepts that are visually represented through semantic or concept maps. (Wood, Lapp, Flood, & Taylor, 2008). Mapping strategies provide students with opportunities to discern similarities, analogies and differences among words (Crovitz & Miller, 2008; Ellery, 2009; Yopp & Yopp, 2007). **Word Maps** can be implemented before, during, and after reading in order to build from students' background knowledge to new concepts, while noting semantic connections and/or differences.

Teacher Modeling and Guiding

1 The teacher begins the lesson by choosing a text that relates to the students social studies unit on justice as it relates to slavery. Many similar articles that can be used for thinking about can be foudn at *www.studentpulse.com/articles/147/2/ nat-turner-and-the-bloodiest-slave-rebellion-in-American-history.*

2 Using a document camera, the teacher shows an article to the students. The teacher points out bolded words as well as headings and subheadings.

3 Thinking aloud, the teacher models how to think about how words connect to one another. "Let's see. Here's the word *secede*. I will list that here at the top of this column. When I think of *secede*, I think of something that doesn't want to be a part of something else. This leads me to think of *antislavery*. I know that *antislavery* relates to *secede* because people who were against slavery didn't want to be a part of slavery. That leads me to think about what those people were called: *abolitionists*. So you can see how all the words in this column relate to one another."

4 After several related words are written in a column the teacher thinks about a label that can describe the entire column. "I think that all these words have something to do with being separate. *Separatists* is a good label for this column."

5 This kind of thinking should continue for the other words and concepts in a unit of study shown in Example 12.1.

Directions: At the top of each column write an important content word from the text or one of your own. In each column write "connecting" words from the text.

Separatists	Disagreements	Oppressed	Faithful
secede	debate	enslaved	allegiance
antislavery	argument	fugitive	dedicated
abolitionists	conflict	captured	honor
independence	disputes	arrested	obey
secession	reject	slavery	obligations

EXAMPLE 12.1. Connections map.

Peer Collaboration and Extension

1 During this time, students work in heterogeneous groups.

2 In groups, students create a connections map of their own on Work Page 12.1 based on a content area being studied.

3 Students write words and draw pictures to help with their understanding of the vocabulary words.

4 Students use chart paper so their work can be posted in the room during a sharing time.

5 As they work, the teacher moves among the students, offering cues and prompts and asking questions that support their performance. For example, if they are creating a chart on the topic of early civilizations of Egypt, Kush, and Mesopotamia, the teacher might prompt them by saying, "To develop your chart, think about comparing the religions, economics, and geography of each civilization." The teacher also makes note of the similar needs existing among the students. This information will help him or her to offer later interventions to students with similar needs.

Teacher Differentiating and Accommodating

Beginning Level

Using teacher-selected content vocabulary (e.g., science unit on plant life), the students and teacher can create a vocabulary chart that illustrates the meaning of the words. Each square contains a title that supports the meaning of the word. Students discuss each word and its meaning, sentences, and where they might encounter the target word (e.g., in a science book, on the playground, in the flower section at the grocery store). Placing each word in multiple contexts helps students fully comprehend the meaning of the word.

EXAMPLE: Vocabulary Word—*flowers*

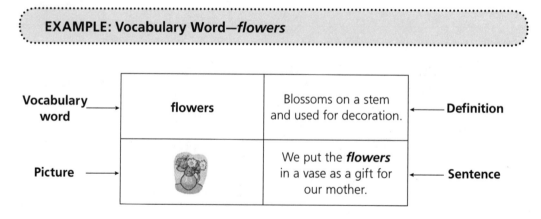

Intermediate Level

Students work in pairs to create vocabulary cards, following the same format used in the vocabulary chart at the beginning level. Students keep the vocabulary cards in a recipe box or on a word ring as a quick reference when writing in the content area. Vocabulary words are kept in alphabetical order for ease of use.

Advanced Level

Working independently, students create vocabulary cards for quick reference during language arts and study in the content areas. Vocabulary cards are expanded to add the antonym and the synonym of each word for further understanding. Homogeneous groups of students are encouraged to share vocabulary cards with one another, discussing the features and possible alternative definitions, antonyms, synonyms, pictures, and sentences.

word	definition	antonym
picture	sentence	synonym

Tech It Out!

Students use Inspiration or Kidspiration software to create word maps or other graphic organizers on individual laptops or classroom computers. Students are encouraged to create folders on their desktops, labeled *content-area study*, so that these word maps and other graphic organizers can be saved for easy reference. Students share their Inspiration-created maps with one another and modify them as needed. For more ways to use Inspiration in the classroom and for a good resource of content-area links, check out *www.internet4classrooms*.

Suggested Websites and Books

www.thinkport.org/technology/template.tp
www.readingrockets.org/strategies/word_maps
enchangedlearning.com/graphicorganizers/vocab

Esbensen, Barbara Juster—*The Night Rainbow* (2000); Scholastic.
Fleischman, Paul—*Seedfolks* (2004); HarperTrophy.
Hesse, Karen—*Out of the Dust* (2001); Klett.
Iwamura, Kazuo—*Where Are You Going? To See My Friend!* (2003); Orchard.
Rawls, Wilson—*Where the Red Fern Grows* (1996); Yearling.

References

Crovitz, D., & Miller, J. A. (2008). Register and charge: Using synonym maps to explore connotation. *English Journal, 97*(4), 49–55.

Ellery, V. (2009). *Creating strategic readers: Techniques for developing competency in phonemic awareness, phonics, fluency, vocabulary, and comprehension* (2nd ed.). Newark, DE: International Reading Association.

Wood, K. D., Lapp, D., Flood, J., & Taylor, D. B. (2008). *Guiding readers through text: Strategy guides for new times* (2nd ed.). Newark, DE: International Reading Association.

Yopp, R., & Yopp, H. (2007). Ten important words plus: A strategy for building word knowledge. *The Reading Teacher, 61*(2), 157–160.

Connections Map

Name: _____

Directions: At the top of each column write an important content word from the text or one of your own. In each column write "connecting" words from the text.

Scaffolding with Text-Supported Information

Common Core Standard

Explain the relationships or interactions between/ among two or more individuals, events, ideas, or concepts in a text by drawing from specific information in the text.

TESOL Standard

Interpret, organize, categorize, and display story or text elements, using visual supports to illustrate description of facts, characters, settings, or events.

Focus skill: Comprehension
Secondary skill: Vocabulary

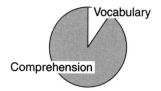

What Is the Purpose?

Support interpretations of a text with information found in the text or related readings.

What Is the Research Base?

Scaffolds are temporary supports that permit learners to participate in a process they may not be able to complete independently (Frey & Fisher, 2010; Klingner, Soltero-González, & Lesaux, 2010; Walqui & van Lier, 2010). *Scaffolding with Text-Supported Information* offers instructional supports to enhance students' oral language, vocabulary development, and comprehension of text as they make text predictions and identify main ideas.

Teacher Modeling and Guiding

1 The teacher begins the lesson by preparing several true–false statements and displays Work Page 13.1 for all to see.

2 The teacher thinks aloud about the first few statements, modeling how he or she thinks about text. "Let's see. Dinosaur bones have been found all over the world. Wow! That seems true, although the world is a big place. I wonder if there are really dinosaur bones in Antarctica or other really cold places. But I do know that there were a lot of dinosaurs, so I am going to put an × on 'True'. That seems true." (See Example 13.1.)

3 The teacher models the first couple of statements in this way, thinking aloud about the validity of each statement.

4 Next, the teacher invites the students to think about whether each statement is true. He or she asks students to share their thinking with a partner.

5 While students discuss the statements in pairs, the teacher listens in to student conversations, guiding and supporting with prompts as necessary. For example, if a pair of students answers yes to a statement about fossils and the teacher realizes they don't understand the word *fossil*, he or she might say, "Let's think about what the word *fossil* means. A fossil is the remains of a plant or animal. Now, thinking about that definition, read that statement again. Do you still think it is true?"

6 Students discuss their predictions and the class comes to a consensus about the statements listed on the chart. If the students cannot agree, a "?" is written on the line following the statement and is revisited during or after reading.

7 After the prediction chart is complete, the teacher reads aloud a text about dinosaurs. As the students listen, they confirm or adjust their previously made predictions.

Make a Prediction	True	False
1. Dinosaur bones have been found all over the world.	X	
2. Dinosaurs walked on land and were also able to swim in the water.		X
3. Scientists believe that land around the world was once all joined together.	X	
4. A fossil is a group of dinosaurs traveling together.		X
5. Scientists have discovered dinosaur footprints in North America.	X	

EXAMPLE 13.1. Completed section of Work Page 13.1.

8 While reading, the teacher models identifying main ideas under the headings and subheadings. The second section of Work Page 13.1 is displayed in front of the students and filled in accordingly.

9 The teacher may say, "I see here that the subheading says, "A Map of the Modern World," and after reading this section I see that the main idea has something to do with scientists believing that dinosaurs lived all over the world. I think I will write that on this chart." (See Example 13.2.)

Peer Collaboration and Extension

1 During this time students work in heterogeneous groups. Students choose a content area text that relates to a whole-class study.

2 Students work collaboratively to complete Work Page 13.1 by making predictions and scanning the text for the main ideas.

3 The teacher prompts students who are struggling as they predict and discuss the main idea of the text. He or she may need to say, "As you read these last two paragraphs, what did you think was the central or main idea? A main idea is what the paragraphs are mostly about. Think about what these paragraphs are mostly about and that will tell you the main idea."

4 Groups of students should be ready to share their Work Pages with other groups so information can be compared across topic areas of study.

Scanning the Text for the Main Idea

Chapter/Story Title: Where Dinosaurs Lived

Headings, Subheadings: A Map of the Modern World

Main Idea: Scientists believe that dinosaurs lived all around the world and traveled by land.

EXAMPLE 13.2. Completed section of Work Page 13.1.

Teacher Differentiating and Accommodating

Beginning Level

The teacher prepares statements (written on sticky notes) or facts from an informational text that will be read aloud. These are placed in a paper bag. After the text is read aloud, the teacher selects and reads aloud a statement or fact from the bag. The students, working in pairs, decide if the statements/facts are true or false and why they believe so. Students place the sticky notes on a teacher created true–false T-chart displayed for all to see (a sample T-chart is shown). Students are encouraged to orally defend why they think a statement/fact is true or false, using textbooks, prior knowledge, the Internet, or other sources. Their ability to do so illustrates their evaluative thinking.

True	False
Alaska is the largest state in the USA.	There are 51 states in the USA.

Intermediate Level

Using a format similar to that given for the beginning level, students work in pairs to decide if the teacher-prepared statements/facts are true or false. If students think a statement/fact is true, they reference on the chart where the statement/fact was found, noting the source and page number, if available.

Advanced Level

In pairs or individually, students create their own true–false statements/facts from informational texts and classroom literature books. Groups of students exchange statements/facts for charting, using the text/literature books for reference. They should note the page on which the true statement was found. Statements changed to the true column when the student provides a true statement and the page number containing the information. Students enjoy debating whether statements are true or false and using their detective skills when searching for evidence to support their claims. By doing so, they illustrate their abilities to synthesize and evaluate information.

True	False
Olivia, a character in several books, is a self-centered pig. (page 4)	

Tech It Out!

Students become Internet detectives as they search websites to locate and support true–false statements for topics they are studying in class. For example, if they are studying an early civilization, true–false statements may include the following:

1. Nomads rarely took tribute payments from agricultural societies, preferring instead to conquer them and assimilate their peoples. *False*

2. Egyptian civilization had more monumental architecture than Mesopotamian. *True*

3. Egyptian civilization did not have the large numbers of slaves and peasants typical of Mesopotamia. *False*

4. The first civilization developed along the banks of the Nile River. *False*

5. Most early civilizations were characterized by the existence of agriculture, main cities, writing systems, and structured states. *True*

6. Monotheism is the belief in a single divinity that was introduced by the Jewish people. *True*

Students decide if a site provides facts or opinions and discuss in small groups whether or not the features of the websites are helpful for research (i.e., banners, pop-ups, photographs, games, audio recordings). Great websites related to early civilizations include:

www.edselect.com/grade52.htm

www.smithlifescience.com/SSEarlyCivilizations.htm

www.socialstudiesforkids.com/subjects/ancientcivilizations.htm

If students are studying U.S. geography, true–false statements might include the following:

1. The Great Lakes that border Canada and the United States are Ontario, Huron, Erie, and Superior. *True*

2. The Mississippi River is the longest river in the world. *False*

3. A large body of water partly surrounded by land is a strait. *False*

4. Latitude is measured east and west of the prime meridian. *False*

5. There are 50 states in the contiguous United States. *False*

6. The North American continent ranks third in land area. *True*

Websites for students about U.S. geography include:

www.sheppardsoftware.com/web_games.htm

wwww.kidport.com/reflib/usageography/usageography.htm

www.gamequarium.com/usgeography.htm

> ### Suggested Websites and Books
>
> *teach.fcps.net/TALK/activities/sniffy_fluffy/MakingPredictions/activity1makingpredictions.htm*
> *www.socialstudiesforkids.com/subjects/geographygames.htm*
> *www.sheppardsoftware.com/European_Geography.htm*
>
> Crook, Connie Brummel—*The Hungry Year* (2001); Fitzhenry and Whiteside.
> Harrison, Troon—*Courage to Fly* (2006); Red Deer Press.
> Seuss, Dr.—*The Foot Book: Dr. Seuss's Wacky Book of Opposites* (1996); Random House Books
>   for Young Readers.
> Stewart, Sarah—*The Journey* (2007); Live Oak Media.
> Wong, Janet—*This Next New Year* (2000); Frances Foster Books.

References

Frey, N., & Fisher, D. (2010). Identifying instructional moves during guided learning. *The Reading Teacher*, 64(2), 84–95.

Klingner, J., Soltero-Gonzalez, L., & Lesaux, N. (2010). RTI for English-language learners. In M. Y. Lipson & K. K. Wixson (Eds.), *Successful approaches to RTI: Collaborative practices for improving K–12 literacy* (pp.). Newark, DE: International Reading Association.

Walqui, A., & van Lier, L. (2010). *Scaffolding the academic success of adolescent English language learners: A pedagogy of promise*. San Francisco: WestEd.

Comprehending the Text

Name: _____

Make a Prediction

		True	False
1.	_____	_____	_____
2.	_____	_____	_____
3.	_____	_____	_____
4.	_____	_____	_____
5.	_____	_____	_____

Scanning the Text for the Main Idea

Chapter/Story Title: _____

Headings, Subheadings: _____

_____

Main Idea: _____

_____

Strategy Lesson 14

Text-Supported Comprehension Guide

Focus skill: Comprehension
Secondary skill: Vocabulary

Common Core Standard
Explicitly draw from context-supported evidence of the topic, text, or issue to probe and reflect on ideas under discussion.

TESOL Standard
Revise thinking or draw conclusions from information in modified grade-level text.

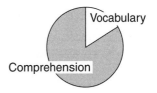

What Is the Purpose?

Use a comprehension guide to support comprehension of text and discussion related to the text information.

What Is the Research Base?

Research demonstrates that reading comprehension can be facilitated when students make personal connections to what they read (Jacobson & Lapp, 2010; Rupley, Blair, & Nichols, 2009; Wood, Pilonieta, & Blanton, 2009). The *Text-Supported Comprehension Guide* provides a systematic, personally relevant approach to text-supported comprehension through analysis. As students engage in guided reading and identifying unfamiliar vocabulary words from books they choose to read independently, they are taught how to return to the text to support their thinking and discussion.

Teacher Modeling and Guiding

1 The teacher begins the lesson by showing students a copy of Work Page 14.1, Text-Supported Comprehension Guide, on a document camera.

2 The teacher thinks aloud as he or she models how to fill in the Text-Supported Comprehension Guide (see Example 14.1). A great text to choose is *Too Many Tamales* by Gary Soto. Beginning with the purpose (Section I), the teacher may say, "We often need to read a story and pay attention to how the actions of the characters and the events relate to our own lives. Making connections helps readers understand what they're reading."

3 "I will add that purpose here." The teacher fills in Section I of the Text-Supported Comprehension Guide. Next, the teacher begins reading, modeling where to list

---

I. My purpose for reading is: <u>To understand the first three pages of the story Too Many Tamales. I plan to write my own story about a traditional celebration in my family.</u>

II. Words I didn't understand:

Paragraph 1	Paragraph 2	Paragraph 3
drifted (floated)	counter (top, tabletop)	kneaded (pressed, blended)
dusk (nightfall)	sticky (gooey, gummy)	apron (outer garment)
glittered (shined)	masa (batter, dough)	thought (to think, believe)

III. Record the most meaningful or interesting information after reading each paragraph.

Paragraph 1

<u>The story takes place during Christmastime. It is snowing outside and lights are shining in the windows.</u>

Paragraph 2

<u>Maria is helping her mother make tamales in the kitchen.</u>

Paragraph 3

<u>Mom has recognized Maria as a grown-up by giving her the responsibility of kneading the masa and letting her wear lipstick and perfume.</u>

EXAMPLE 14.1. Teacher-completed Work Page 14.1.

words that are unfamiliar (Section II). While the teacher lists these words, he or she might indicate how he or she may have heard the words before but can't quite understand them in this context.

4 After each paragraph, the teacher fills in Section III of the Text-Supported Comprehension Guide. He or she thinks aloud something like "Hmm. After reading this first paragraph, what might I find to be the most meaningful or interesting information?" After reading paragraph 2 the teacher might say, "I think this information about Maria in paragraph 2 is interesting. It also relates to my purpose and focus of paying attention to the characters as I read. Going back to the story always helps me to check my thoughts about what I am reading."

5 The teacher continues to model his or her thinking, returning often to the Text-Supported Comprehension Guide to record his or her thoughts. The teacher also emphasizes how the information he or she is charting is based on the inferences drawn while reading the text and in returning to the text to check his or her thinking.

Peer Collaboration and Extension

1 During this time, students work in heterogeneous groups.

2 The students in a group read a short text, perhaps three paragraphs, and complete Work Page 14.1 together. Choosing short articles from the Internet is helpful for this strategy.

3 Each student in the group is responsible for orally contributing to the content of what is written on the Work Page. However, each student contributes by leading the discussion about each of the different sections in the Text-Supported Comprehension Guide. For example, one student is responsible for leading a discussion about words that are confusing (Section II), and another student is responsible for leading the discussion about the most meaningful information in paragraph 1 (Section III), etc.

4 As they work, the teacher moves among the students, offering cues and prompts and asking questions that support their performance. For example, the teacher might say, "I see this word is confusing for you. Where have you heard the word before? Let's look together and see if we can understand this word within the context of the sentence you are reading." The teacher also makes note of the similar needs existing among the students. This information can help the teacher to offer later interventions to students with similar needs.

5 The division of roles helps the students to stay on task and hold each other accountable for completing the task.

Teacher Differentiating and Accommodating

From the information the teacher gained as students worked collaboratively, he or she is now able to offer instruction that provides guided interventions to students with similar needs. As the teacher does so, the others read texts similar to those listed as suggested books or are engaged with the Tech It Out! activity. They may also continue having text-based discussions that are supported by information they noted on their Text-Supported Comprehension Guide.

Beginning Level

During or after a read-aloud or shared reading, each of the students creates an interactive graphic organizer that supports comprehension, sequencing, and retelling. Using the flip-book format from the *Big Book of Books and Activities* by Dinah Zike (Dinah-Might Activities, 1992), students are able to relate the elements of a story, such as character, setting, problem, and solution. In each section, the students draw a picture and add a key vocabulary word or words to support and illustrate their comprehension. They then use these to support their discussion of the text.

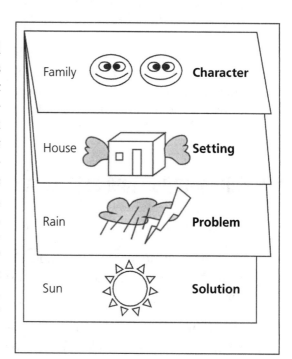

Intermediate Level

Using the same interactive graphic organizer as at the beginning level, each of the students constructs a sentence in each section to support their comprehension. Pictures can be added for additional support (e.g., The setting is in a house in the middle of a dark, spooky forest). As sentences are shared in a small- or whole-group setting, students also note how the ideas are related to the book they are reading.

Advanced Level

Using only one element from a story (e.g., the characters), each student creates a new setting, problem, and solution. The students record each element in the appropriate sections of the flip book, using key vocabulary words and pictures. They share their original stories and flip books with their partners and then share with the whole class. They note the similarities between the book they have read and the story they have written.

Tech It Out!

After reading or writing a text, students download related clip-art photos, charts, graphics, maps, and so on, from appropriate websites on the Internet, to include in flip books and Text-Supported Comprehension Guides. Text-Supported Comprehension Guides can be stored on computer desktops so that students can take notes by keyboarding rather than using a paper and pencil. For free clip art, pictures, photographs, and illustrations, try *classroomclipart.com/cgi-bin/kids/imageFolio.cgi?direct=Clipart/Maps*.

Suggested Websites and Books

www.learnnc.org/lp/external/5461
www.nea.org/tools/18347.htm
edhelper.com/ReadingComprehension.htm

Anaya, Rudolfo—*Bless Me Ultima* (1999); Warner Books.
Edelman, Bernard (Ed.)—*Dear America: Letters Home from Vietnam* (2002); W. W. Norton.
Levy, Janice—*The Spirit of Tio Fernando: A Day of the Dead Story* (1995); Albert Whitman & Company.
New Rider Weber, EdNah—*Rattlesnake Mesa* (2004); Lee & Low Books.
Wilhelm, Hans—*Hello Sun!* (2003); First Avenue Editions.

References

Jacobson, J., & Lapp, D. (2010). Modeling writing to enhance students' critical and creative thinking skills. *The California Reader, 43*(3), 32–47.

Rupley, W. H., Blair, T. R., & Nichols, W. D. (2009). Effective reading instruction for struggling readers: The role of direct/explicit teaching. *Reading and Writing Quarterly, 25*(2–3), 125–139.

Wood, K. D., Pilonieta, P., & Blanton, W. E. (2009). Teaching content and skills through integrated literacy circles. *Middle School Journal, 41*(1), 56–62.

Text-Supported Comprehension Guide

Name: _____

I. My purpose for reading is: _____

_____

II. Words I didn't understand:

Paragraph 1	Paragraph 2	Paragraph 3
_____	_____	_____
_____	_____	_____
_____	_____	_____
_____	_____	_____

III. Record the most meaningful or interesting information after reading each paragraph.

Paragraph 1

_____

_____

_____

_____

Paragraph 2

_____

_____

_____

_____

Paragraph 3

_____

_____

_____

_____

Visualizing Steps in a Process

Common Core Standard

Report on a topic or text, tell a story, or recount an experience in an organized, sequential manner, using appropriate facts and relevant, descriptive details to support main ideas or themes; speak clearly at an understandable pace.

TESOL Standard

Identify and order main ideas and details, using modified grade-level stories and texts.

Focus skill: Comprehension
Secondary skill: Pronunciation for Discussion

What Is the Purpose?

Use illustrations to identify steps in a process or sequence within a story.

What Is the Research Base?

Students need to be taught to use precise language and images to convey their thinking (Lapp, Fisher, & Johnson, 2010). Writing supported with illustrations encourages students to contemplate and express ideas related to text material in the target language as well as to try different constructions to make themselves understood (Dreher & Gray, 2009; Frey & Fisher, 2010; Norman, 2010). *Visualizing Steps in a Process* provides a context that encourages students to develop a visual image of what they have read in a text to support their understanding of the sequence or steps in a process or story structure.

Teacher Modeling and Guiding

1 The teacher starts the lesson by choosing a text that has a step-by-step process that is explained clearly.

2 The book *From Seed to Plant* by Allan Fowler works well for this strategy, as teachers can model the growth process.

3 The teacher begins by reading the first step in a process. The teacher then thinks aloud, highlighting the words he or she has read. "Let's see. 'First, you must plant the seeds.' I see the word *first* so I know it is the number one thing that must happen. I am imagining my grandmother and me putting seeds in the ground in her backyard. I will draw a picture of that here." The teacher draws a sketch of planting seeds on Work Page 15.1.

4 As the teacher continues this modeling it is important to focus on the steps in the process but also on the *language* that is being used to describe the process. Signal words, such as *first*, *second*, *next*, *then*, and *last*, are especially helpful as students comprehend text that has a temporal structure.

5 The teacher may also wish to make an academic word bank on chart paper so students can refer to the language that is expected of them (see below).

6 After each sketch in the process, the teacher models how to write a couple of words next to the sketch.

**How a Plant Grows
Word Bank**

First	Next	Last
Second	After	In the end
Third	Finally	
Fourth	After	
Fifth	Then	

Peer Collaboration and Extension

1 During this time, students work in heterogeneous groups.

2 The teacher and the students as a whole class create and chart a list of activities that include a sequence of events such as tying shoes, getting ready for school, reading a recipe, steps in a science experiment, events leading to a historical incident.

If they are unable to think of others, the teacher might share a favorite comic strip or read *The Watsons Go to Birmingham: 1963* by Christopher Paul Curtis. This is a historical fiction text written in 1995 that offers a sequence of historical events experienced by an ordinary family.

3 Students, as partners or in small groups, then select one of the events and work together completing Work Page 15.1 as a group.

4 As they work, the teacher moves among the students, offering cues and prompts and asking questions that support their performance. The teacher makes note of the similar needs existing among the students. This information can help him or her to offer later interventions to students with similar needs. For example, as students work together, the teacher listens for the use of *first, second, next, then, last,* or other signal words that help students describe steps in a process. If they are not using these academic language markers, the teacher again models using them.

5 Teams complete Work Page 15.1 or reproduce their sketches and words on chart paper to be shared with the whole class.

Teacher Differentiating and Accommodating

From the information the teacher gained as students worked collaboratively, he or she is now able to offer instruction that provides guided interventions to students with similar needs. As the teacher does so, the others read texts similar to those listed as suggested books or can be engaged with the Tech It Out! activity. They can also continue illustrating a sequence on a second topic selected from those charted on the list created with the teacher.

Beginning Level

Using the signal words, *first, second, third,* and *last,* the teacher models the steps in making a sandwich (other examples include brushing teeth, tying shoes). The teacher shares with the class premade sentences (written on sentence strips) that coordinate with each step in the process. Students are asked to insert the correct signal word (also written on sentence strips) that corresponds to the correct step. Students read the signal word and the sentence that corresponds with it. Reading aloud several of the steps may be necessary to aid in comprehension of the text.

First	Take two slices of bread from the bag of bread.
Second	Spread peanut butter on one slice.
Third	Spread jelly on the other piece of bread.
Last	Put bread together, slice in half, and eat.

Intermediate Level

The teacher demonstrates how to make/do something, using specific steps (e.g., how to make ice cubes). The students work in pairs, and collaborate to create and sketch their ideas in small squares on paper. The squares of paper are then given to another group to sequence and add sentences with signal words.

Advanced Level

In pairs or small groups, students create their own "how to" writing, using signal words (e.g., *first, next, then, last, finally*). Students present their sentences orally to the class, mixing up the order. Class members try to determine which sentence should come first, which should come second, and so on. Instead of creating their own writing, students may use a text such as *The Kite Rider* by Geraldine McCaughrean. This is a great activity to develop oral language, auditory memory, and listening comprehension.

Tech It Out!

To help visualize steps in a process and sequence information, students create an electronic storybook using iWork, Microsoft Word, KidPix, or another program that has a slide show or presentation function. To create a slide show, students simply create a word processed document. Each individual page becomes a separate slide. Student-created drawings and digital photographs can be included in the slide show along with the vocabulary that illustrates the sequencing pattern. For more ideas, check out *www.members.tripod.com/hamminkj/technology.html*.

Suggested Websites and Books

www.chicanolitbib.wordpress.com/2007
www.childrensbookpress.org
www.proteacher.org/c/729_Sequence.html

Benjamin, Michelle—*Constellations: Twenty Years of Stellar Poetry from Polestar* (2003); Raincoast Books.
Gilchrist, Cherry—*A Calendar of Festivals* (2005); Barefoot Books.
Katz, Karen—*I Can Share: A Lift-the-Flap Book* (2004); Grosset & Dunlap.
Saenz, Benjamin Alire—*A Gift from Papa Diego* (1998); Cinco Puntos Press.
Thien, Madeleine—*The Chinese Violin* (2001); Walrus Books.

References

Dreher, M. J., & Gray, J. L. (2009). Compare, contrast, comprehend: Using compare–contrast text structures with ELLs in K–3 classrooms. *The Reading Teacher, 63*(2), 132–141.

Frey, N., & Fisher, D. (2010). Reading and the brain: What early childhood educators need to know. *Early Childhood Education Journal, 38*(2), 103–110.

Lapp, D., Fisher, D., & Johnson, K. (2010). Text mapping plus: Improving comprehension through supported retellings. *Journal of Adolescent and Adult Literacy, 53*(5), 423–426.

Norman, R. R. (2010). Picture this: Processes prompted by graphics in informational text. *Literacy Teaching and Learning, 14*(1–2), 1–39.

Steps in a Process

Name: _____

It's your turn to "Describe the Process."
Be prepared to share your pictures with a partner.

Step 1

_____

_____

_____

_____

_____

Step 2

_____

_____

_____

_____

_____

Step 3

_____

_____

_____

_____

_____

What does your partner like most about your illustrations?

_____

_____

_____

Text-Supported Conversations

Common Core Standard

Participate in small- and larger-group collaborative conversations with diverse partners about grade-level topics and texts.

TESOL Standard

Discuss and summarize current critical issues using visual or graphic supports.

Focus skill: Comprehension
Secondary skill: Fluency in Speaking and Reading

Fluency in Speaking and Reading

Comprehension

What Is the Purpose?

Identify a question, fact, or other meaningful event from a text and use text-based evidence to support discussion.

What Is the Research Base?

Conversations about text-based literature and facts positively affect literacy development (Gorsuch & Taguchi, 2010; Liang & Galda, 2009; Zwiers, 2004). The *Reflect and Respond Question Guide* included in this lesson serves as an organizational tool for thoughtful class discussions. The responses, as well as the inquiries, are used as an avenue to foster repeated reading, extended contemplation of text-based material, and oral language skill development.

Teacher Modeling and Guiding

1 The teacher begins the lesson by showing students a copy of Work Page 16.1, the Reflect and Respond Question Guide, on a document camera explaining that he or she uses this guide to list important pieces of information and questions he or she might have while reading. The teacher explains that he or she then uses both the information and the questions to help with writing or conversing about the text.

2 After reading several pages of a challenging text, the teacher models thinking aloud about a question, important fact, or something that is particularly meaningful from the text.

3 For example, if the teacher were reading Shakespeare's *Romeo and Juliet* with an eighth-grade English class, he or she may say, "Hmm. An important fact from the story? Let's see, the two families that were feuding are named Montague and Capulet. That's a fact from the text, and I learned that from page 1. I will write that here in this column and write the page number in this column." She might also say, "I wonder why they were fighting?" As she talks, she writes Why? On the chart. The teacher may continue this kind of thinking with one or two more examples.

4 Then the teacher asks students to form as partners or small groups to read, discuss, and chart their responses, questions, and page numbers.

5 The teacher also invites the students to add their names to the first column of the chart. She adds her name to the statements she modeled.

6 Next, the teacher explains how to add the concluding statement to the lower portion of the Work Page. In groups, students take the information from the top of the Work Page and write a concluding statement.

7 When finished, each team presents its charted information and the questions that are discussed.

Example 16.1 shows what a completed Work Page might look like after students read the text of *Romeo and Juliet*.

Student	Page	Response/Question
Student	1	The two families that were feuding are named Montague and Capulet. Why?
Student	2	The servants had been fighting.
Samantha	1	The prince warned both sides not to disturb the peace.
Guillermo	3	I don't understand the line: "Love is a smoke made with the fume of sighs."
Fernando	1	No one could remember why the quarreling had begun.
Jessica	2	What does this line mean: "He has been this way much of late."
Daniel	3	Benvolio tells Romeo that Rosaline will be at a dance that night at the home of the Capulets.

Groups by Page Numbers

Page 1

Student: The two families that were feuding are named Montague and Caplulet.

Samantha: The prince warned both sides not to disturb the peace.

Fernando: No one could remember why the quarreling had begun.

Concluding Statements: A fight between the Montague and Capulet families had continued

for many years but no one could remember how it started.

Page 2

Student: The servants had been fighting.

Jessica: What does this line mean: "He has been this way much of late."

Concluding Statements: The servants had been fighting in the town square.

Romeo's parents were looking for hime.

Page 3

Guillermo: I don't understand the line "Love is a smoke made with the fume of sighs."

Daniel: Benvolio tells Romeo that Rosaline will be at a dance that night at the home of the

Capulets.

Concluding Statements: Romeo knows that Rosaline does not love him, but he decides to

go to the dance for a chance to see her.

EXAMPLE 16.1. Completed Work Page 16.1.

Peer Collaboration and Extension

1 During this time, students work in small heterogeneous groups.

2 Students next complete a Reflect and Respond Question Guide in small groups, using a text they have all read. This can be a text read in a book club or literature circle or a chapter from a textbook.

3 As the students work, the teacher moves among them offering cues and prompts and asking questions that support their performance. For example, when a student is unclear about a language phrase such as *this way much of late* in the sentence *He has been this way much of late*, the teacher supplies the meaning because the lack of clarity is interfering with comprehension and conversation. The teacher also makes note of the similar needs existing among the students. This information can help the teacher to offer later interventions to students with similar needs.

4 During the discussion, students are asked to note additional questions and comments that occurred to them in whole-class and small-group discussions.

5 Teachers may create a more supported activity sheet for English learners at the beginning level or may challenge students who are working at the intermediate level. Work Page 16.2 for beginning level English learners and Work Page 16.3 for students at the intermediate level can be used to support these students. For Work Page 16.2, prepare a summary cloze (fill in the blank) activity sheet for a selected text with two possible choices to complete each sentence. Invite students to read the first paragraph from the text aloud to students. Then read the cloze (fill-in) sentences. Ask students to volunteer answers that can complete the sentences. For Work Page 16.3, after reading a text such as *Martin's Big Words: The Life of Dr. Martin Luther King Jr.* by Rappaport, invite students to write a letter to the author. Explain to students that this is their personal response letter to the author and that the "Talking to the Author" guide will prove them with a means to express ideas that can be of interest to the author.

Teacher Differentiating and Accommodating

From the information the teacher gained as students worked collaboratively, he or she is now able to offer instruction that provides guided interventions to students with similar needs. As the teacher does so, the others can read texts similar to those listed as suggested books or can be engaged with the Tech It Out! activity. They can also continue having text-supported discussions that are supported by information they noted on the Reflect and Response Guide.

Beginning Level

The teacher creates a model of a Jeopardy! game, using categories selected from the content/topic being studied. Answers consist of questions generated during a read-aloud or shared reading with the whole class or small group, or by students during independent reading. Students answer in a question form. The following example includes literature studied in a fifth-grade class.

> **Example: Category—*Harvesting Hope* (Krull, 2003) for $100**
>
> **Answer**—Central California
>
> **Question**—"Where did the march take place?"
>
> The teacher provides question stems (*who, what, where, when, why,* and *how*). Students work in teams or partners, talking through their questions/answers.

Intermediate Level

Using the same format as the in beginning-level activity, students work independently, using question stems if needed. If there is a discrepancy with the students' answers, further discussion occurs.

Advanced Level

Following the Jeopardy! game format, students create their own game (i.e., write questions and answers), using information gained from independent reading, shared reading, or read-aloud lessons. Students are reminded to say each answer in the form of a question. Students can be heterogeneously grouped and compete with one another.

Jeopardy! Game Example

Harvesting Hope	Lon Po Po	The Quilt Story	Romeo and Juliet	Martin's Big Words
$100 Central California	$100 Little Red Riding Hood	$100 Wagon	$100 William Shakespeare	$100 Civil Rights Leader
$200 Huelga	$200 China	$200 Change and Continuity	$200 Capulet	$200 1955
$300 La Causa	$300 Yeh-Shen	$300 Tomie dePaola	$300 Montague	$300 Doreen Rappaport
$400 Helen	$400 Granny Wolf	$400 Tony Johnston	$400 Feuding	$400 Rosa Parks

Tech It Out!

Using a game software program, Vuvox, PowerPoint, or a web page design application such as Dreamweaver, students create a digital Jeopardy! game board. Students or teams of students construct their game with "hot links" that will connect to answers or questions. The teacher projects the game in class for whole-class participation or sets up the game on a computer for small groups to use at a learning center. For a variety of Jeopardy! games focused on buoyancy, presidents, and phonics, try *www.surfnetkids.com/games/Triia_Games.*

Suggested Websites and Books

www.ala.org/ala/mgrps/divs/alsc/awardsgrants/bookmedia/belpremedal/index.cfm
abcteach.com/directory/reading_comprehension
www.a4esl.org (quizzes for ELLs)

Dolan, Marlena—*Just Talking About Ourselves: Voices of Our Youth*, vol. 3 (1997); Theytus Books.
Eastman, Charles A.—*Indian Heroes and Great Chieftains* (2010); Nabu Press.
Jones, Ron—*The Acorn People* (1996); Laurel Leaf.
Sekaquaptewa, Emory; & Pepper, Barbara—*Coyote & the Winnowing Birds: A Traditional Hopi Tale* (1994); Clear Light Books.
Sutherland, Margaret; & Lamut, Sonja—*Thanksgiving Is for Giving Thanks* (2000); Grosset & Dunlap.

References

Gorsuch, G., & Taguchi, E. (2010). Developing reading fluency and comprehension using repeated reading: Evidence from longitudinal student reports. *Language Teaching Research, 14*(1), 27–59.

Liang, L. A., & Galda, L. (2009). Responding and comprehending: Reading with delight and understanding. *The Reading Teacher, 63*(4), 330–333.

Zwiers, J. (2004). *Developing academic thinking skills in grades 6–12: A handbook of multiple intelligence activities.* Newark, DE: International Reading Association.

Reflect and Respond Question Guide

Student	Page	Response/Question

Groups by Page Numbers

Page 1

Student: _____

_____

Concluding Statements: _____

_____

Page 2

Student: _____

_____

Concluding Statements: _____

_____

Page 3

Student: _____

_____

Concluding Statements: _____

_____

Romeo and Juliet

Students fill in sentences taken directly from the text. (Answers are in parentheses.)

1. The Montagues and the Capulets were two families who often _____ _____ (quarreled, celebrated) with one another.

2. The prince tells the boys that he wants a _____ (peaceful, powerful) village.

3. When Benvolio tells Romeo that Rosaline will be at the party, he then shows _____ _____ . (sadness, interest)

4. Juliet's mother wants to know if she can love the _____ _____ (young, honorable) Count Paris.

5. Juliet's nurse tries to _____ for her. (question, answer)

6. On the way to the dance, Romeo tells his friends that he is a _____ _____ dancer. (talented, poor)

7. Romeo looks into the night sky and he _____. (shudders, shouts)

8. Romeo states that he believes that attending the dance will result in having to suffer some type of _____ . (compliment, consequence)

9. "I will not be a _____!" shouts Romeo. (coward, villain)

10. As Romeo searches for Rosaline, his eyes catch _____ of the fair Juliet. (sight, light)

Talking to the Author Guide

Dear _____

I recently finished reading your book _____

_____

The most interesting part of your book is _____

_____

I think that other people would find this interesting also because _____

_____

By reading your book, I learned _____

_____

As I was reading, I was thinking about _____

_____

I would like to ask you _____

_____

The reason I ask this question is _____

_____

_____

I think that the best part of your book is _____

_____

Thank you very much for reading my letter. _____

_____

_____

_____

_____

_____

_____

Sincerely, _____

Knowing How to Comprehend a Text

Common Core Standard

Cite the textual evidence that most strongly supports an analysis of what the text says explicitly as well as inferences drawn from the text.

TESOL Standard

Skim visually or graphically supported text to confirm or verify information.

Focus skill: Comprehension
Secondary skill: Reading and Language Fluency

Reading and Language Fluency

Comprehension

What Is the Purpose?

Identify reading strategies and text structures that are supportive of understanding a text.

What Is the Research Base?

Proficient readers do not use skills in isolation. They in fact bundle or use many simultaneously (Pressley, 2001). Providing students with interesting, engaging texts and tasks can facilitate their comprehension of reading content (Frye, Trathen, & Wilson, 2009; Gambrell, Morrow, Pressley, & Guthrie, 2007). My Reading Log (Work Page 17.1) can be used in all content areas as students endeavor to grasp the academic concepts throughout the curriculum. There are two sections: *Reading Strategies*, which encourages students to identify and explain the cognitive skills they use while reading, and *Text Structures*, which supports analysis of the type of structure or patterns used by the author of the text. The end goal is enhanced language and comprehension.

Teacher Modeling and Guiding

1 The teacher selects a familiar story or textbook passage to review and model through a think-aloud example of reading comprehension strategies and text structure with the students (Example 17.1).

2 Before reading a story or chapter from the text, the teacher provides each student with a copy of Work Page 17.1.

3 While modeling thinking, the teacher says, "Let's see. What strategies am I using as I read this text? As I look at these subheadings on page 39, I predict that I will be reading about solving word problems. This subheading gives me that clue."

4 After modeling one or two reading strategies and recording them on the Work Page, the teacher invites students to work in cooperative groups to complete one or two.

5 Once the teacher is sure students have an understanding of how to record their thinking and show evidence of where they obtained the information, he or she models the same process, using text structures.

6 The teacher may say, "Hmm. I see these words here on page 40. It looks like these words are explaining something to me. Now, I know what *adding*, *subtracting*, *multiplying*, and *dividing* mean. This is a text structure that describes or explains something, so I will put it here next to the word "descriptive."

Note: This lesson may be taught across 2 days. Teachers may wish to spend 1 day focusing on reading strategies and the other day on text structures.

Peer Collaboration and Extension

1 During this time, students work in heterogeneous groups to complete the Reading Log that was begun in the whole-group lesson.

2 As they work, the teacher moves among the students, offering cues and prompts and asking questions that support their performance. The teacher may need to offer some guidance and support for some groups of students. He or she may say, "What strategy are you using? What is going through your mind as you think about the words on the page? Are you imagining a picture in your head as you read that? If so, that is visualizing."

3 The teacher also makes note of the similar needs existing among the students. This information will help him or her to offer later interventions to students with similar needs.

Name: Javier   Story/Text: Basic Math (Chapter 3)   Date: 10/04

Title: Solving Word Problems

Reading Strategies

Reading Strategy	Page	Example
Predicting	39	As I look at the subheadings, I predict that I'll be reading about how to solve word problems.
Visualizing, Using Imagery	39	I see a car traveling 50 miles per hour on a highway and a train rushing down shiny train tracks traveling 75 miles per hour.
Monitoring Comprehension	39	I understand that first I must think about what is being asked and then underline and list the information given in the problem.
Clarifying	39	I need to clarify the word equation by using the glossary.
Inferencing	40	When I see the question, is all the given information necessary to solve the problem? I think that the problem might contain extra information.
Organizing, Classifying	40	Numbers 1–4 are pre-equation formulation strategies. Numbers 5–7 are during equation formulation strategies.
Summarizing	40	To solve word problems I need to identify information and visualize the problem.
Analyzing	40	I think that the explanation was similar to the steps in a recipe.
Evaluating	40	I think that the steps I read about will be helpful.

Text Structures

	Page	Example
Descriptive	40	The words that are used to indicate adding, subtracting, multiplying, and dividing in word problems are explained.
Sequence	39	I read a sequence of strategies to solve word problems.
Cause–Effect	43	Finding the interest gained after a deposit of $1,000.
Comparison–Contrast	42	Contrast the time needed to type 60 with typing 25 pages. (ratio)
Problem–Solution	44	If Tim hires Bill and Tom, how fast can they both mow the lawn?
Fact–Opinion	39	All the information provided is factual.
Chronological Order	44	In 1985 Arnold's salary rose 15%. In 1984, he earned $30,000.
Enumeration, Steps	39	The author explains the strategies in a seven-step list.

EXAMPLE 17.1. Completed Work Page 17.1.

Teacher Differentiating and Accommodating

From the information the teacher gained as students worked collaboratively, he or she is now able to offer instruction that provides guided interventions to students with similar needs. As the teacher does so, the others can read texts similar to those listed as suggested books or can be engaged with the Tech It Out! activity. They can also continue having text-supported discussions that are supported by information they noted on the Reading Log.

Beginning Level

Two groups of students are needed for a fishbowl activity—one group (consisting of about four or five students) to converse inside the circle and one group (the rest of the class) to sit around the outside of the circle, "listening in" on the conversation. The inside group discusses the text from the shared reading or read-aloud lesson. Students in the inside circle help one another make meaning, asking questions, predicting, summarizing, and so on. Students in the inner circle can refer to the text, helping each other clarify confusing parts of the text. After the inner-circle discussion is complete, students in the outside circle can further help by prompting, clarifying, and asking questions. The inner circle of students can serve as a model for the other students as they "think aloud" the text.

Intermediate Level

Students make a flip-strip Foldable as a note-taking guide (see Example 17.2). The reading strategy or text structure is written on the outside, and an example is written on the inside of each flap. Students refer to this aid as they read so that they become more cognitively aware of the strategies and text structures they encounter while reading.

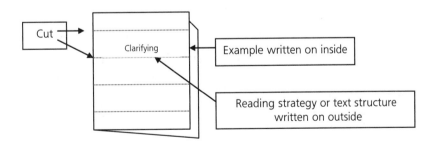

EXAMPLE 17.2. Flip-strip Foldable.

Advanced Level

Using words from their reading logs, students develop a *found poem* that can be shared with a partner. For additional information on creating found poems, visit *www.educationoasis.com/curriculum/LP/LA/creating_found_poetry.htm*. The following is an example of a found poem developed from a student's Reading Log entry after reading about the California gold rush in the book *Gold Fever* by Verla Kay:

> Westward Wagon Trains,
> Excited Family
> Headlines Screaming Gold
> Levi Jeans
> Panning, Mines, Opportunities,
> Westward Dreams

Tech It Out!

The teacher creates a blog (web log) that poses an essential question or prompt relating to a book or content being studied. Such questions and prompts should be intriguing, inviting students to respond to the questions and write new wonderings of their own while responding or relating to the wonderings of peers. For example, if students are reading *Charlie and the Chocolate Factory* by Roald Dahl, the teacher may pose this question: "So many of the characters in this book are considered obnoxious. Why would they be deserving of the Golden Ticket?" Students can respond to the question in a blog and pose new wonderings they may have about the book. Students who are blogging wizards should be encouraged to work with less-proficient bloggers. To learn more about using blogs in the classroom, check out *classblogmeister.com*, and for a discussion on blogging in education, see *weblogs. about.com/od/usesandrolesofblogs/a/weblogged.htm*.

Suggested Websites and Books

wwww.reading.org
www.nea.org
www.englishlearner.com/tests

Debon, Nicolas—*A Brave Soldier* (2002); Groundwood Books.
Duncan, Barbara—*Origin of the Milky Way* (2010); The University of North Carolina Press.
Mahmoody, Betty—*Not without My Daughter* (1991); St. Martin's Paperbacks.
Rosa-Mendoza, Gladys—*When I Am/Cuando estoy* (2007); me+mi publishing.
Wiesel, Elie—*Night* (2006); Hill and Wang.

References

Frye, E. M., Trathen, W., & Wilson, K. (2009). Pirates in historical fiction and nonfiction: A twin-text unit of study. *Social Studies and the Young Learner, 21*(3), 15–16.

Gambrell, L. B., Morrow, L. M., Pressley, M., & Guthrie, J. T. (Eds.). (2007). *Best practices in literacy instruction* (3rd ed.). New York: Guilford Press.

Pressley, M. (2001). Comprehension instruction: What makes sense now, what might make sense soon. *Reading Online, 5*(2). Available at *www.readingonline.org/articles/art_ index.asp?HREF=handbook/pressley/index.html.*

My Reading Log

Name: _____ Story/Text: _____ Date: _____

Title: _____

Reading Strategies

Reading Strategy	Page	Example
Predicting		
Visualizing, Using Imagery		
Monitoring Comprehension		
Clarifying		
Inferencing		
Organizing, Classifying		
Summarizing		
Analyzing		
Evaluating		

Text Structures

	Page	Example
Descriptive		
Sequence		
Cause–Effect		
Comparison–Contrast		
Problem–Solution		
Fact–Opinion		
Chronological Order		
Enumeration, Steps		

Talking about Text
The Peer Tutoring Guide

Common Core Standard

Interpret information presented in diverse media and formats (e.g., visually, quantitatively, orally) and explain how it contributes to a topic, text, or issue under study.

TESOL Standard

Initiate or engage in text-related conversations with peers or in small groups.

Focus skill: Comprehension
Secondary skill: Vocabulary for Conversation

Vocabulary for Conversation

Comprehension

What Is the Purpose?

Identify and paraphrase information in the text to help peers understand.

What Is the Research Base?

Collaboration should involve (1) the integration of oral language development, reading, and writing throughout all phases of instruction and (2) the use of higher-order thinking and social skills (Bauer, Manyak, & Cook, 2010; Ogle & Correa-Kovtun, 2010; Van Keer & Vanderlinde, 2010). Peer and cross-age tutoring experiences can provide purposeful, authentic contexts for ELLs to hear and practice the target language related to texts they are reading and writing. The *Peer Tutoring Guide* is an outline for partner work that can be used within self-contained classrooms in all content areas.

Teacher Modeling and Guiding

1 The teacher displays Work Page 18.1, Peer Tutoring Guide, for students to see.

2 To begin, the teacher shows the students how to complete the information at the top of the guide by identifying the course, the teacher's name, the name of the student who is acting as the tutor, the name of the partner, the goal, date, and pages to read. Then, after reading the identified pages about how climate conditions have affected agriculture in China, the teacher may think aloud about any words or main ideas that are confusing.

3 Next, using Example 18.1, the teacher models how to think about the text in terms of the guiding phrases shown on the Peer Tutoring Guide. For example, after reading the first phrase, which says, "What I don't understand," the teacher might say, "Gosh, this is confusing. I really don't understand what these paragraphs are about. I am not understanding the main ideas. The words that are confusing to me are *plateau, Huang, levees*." The teacher then models how to write this information on the first line. He or she might write, "I don't understand the main idea of the paragraphs. These words are difficult for me: *plateau, Huang, levees*."

4 The teacher then asks the class to explain the information to her. Once the students finish, he or she writes their clarification into the Guide.

5 The teacher partners students and invites them to work as peer tutors for each other to make sense of what they are reading.

6 Ask students to work together to complete the Guide on Work Page 18.1 and to include a product (e.g., the beginning of an essay, answers to a tutor's questions, end-of-chapter questions related to their reading, written personal responses to selected books). (See Example 18.1.)

Peer Collaboration and Extension

1 During this time, students work in heterogeneous partner teams to complete the Peer Tutoring Guide. As they work, the teacher moves among them offering cues and prompts and asking questions that support their performance. For example, when listening to various partners the teacher might offer prompts such as, "What is confusing for you here? Think carefully as I reread this sentence with you. Look again at the information in the chart. What is the author showing with this picture? Now, what might the words under the picture say?"

2 The teacher may need to change partner teams if the kind of peer support needed is not available from the students acting as tutors.

3 In addition, the teacher makes note of the similar needs existing among the students. This information can help him or her to offer later interventions to students with similar needs.

Course: <u>World History</u>   Teacher: <u>Ms. Horton</u>   Date: <u>10/08/11</u>

Tutor: <u>Jessica</u>   Partner: <u>Veronica</u>

Goal: <u>Review Chapter 7 to understand how climatic conditions have affected agriculture</u>
<u>in China.</u>

Pages to Read: <u>Pages 160–163</u>

After Reading:

1. What I don't understand (e.g., words, a main idea, a process): <u>I don't understand the main</u>
   <u>idea of the paragraphs. These words are difficult:</u>
   <u>plateau, Huang, levees.</u>

2. What my partner explained: <u>A plateau is a raised section of land and that many of Asia's</u>
   <u>largest rivers begin on this plateau. Huang is the name of one of the large rivers in</u>
   <u>China. A levee is a wall that keeps a river from overflowing. My partner explained that</u>
   <u>when the water from the river goes down, silt deposits remain. This is a type of</u>
   <u>rock-free fertile soil that can enrich farmlands and crops.</u>

3. Three examples of what we practiced: <u>Think About It Questions Page 163</u>
   a. <u>The Huang River and the Indus River are both large rivers that begin on Asia's</u>
      <u>largest plateau.</u>
   b. <u>"Loess" is a dusty, yellow soil that helps farmers because it provides fertile soil,</u>
      <u>but it is easily carried away by storms, leaving farmers with poor soil.</u>
   c. <u>It was important for ancient farmers to control the Huang River because their</u>
      <u>fields could have been washed away.</u>

4. What I now better understand: <u>I understand that the soil surrounding the Huang River</u>
   <u>can provide nutrients to the soil, but that if the river overflows due to heavy rains,</u>
   <u>farmers' crops can be destroyed.</u>

5. Attached are my completed products: <u>Jessica is helping me copy the map of China on</u>
   <u>page 161. We will include the names of the geographical regions and rivers. Then we're</u>
   <u>going to read You Read to Me. I'll Read to You: Very Short Stories to Read Together.</u>

EXAMPLE 18.1. Completed Work Page 18.1.

Teacher Differentiating and Accommodating

From the information the teacher gained as students worked collaboratively, he or she is now able to offer instruction that provides guided interventions to students with similar needs. As the teacher does so, the others can read texts similar to those listed as suggested books or can be engaged with the Tech It Out! activity. They can also continue having text-supported discussions that are supported by information they noted on their Peer Tutoring Guide.

Beginning Level

The teacher invites students to think of this activity as if they were creating a book trailer, much like a movie trailer we see when we go to the movies and watch previews of upcoming shows. Working with a peer, each student creates an oral presentation supported by related realia that can be mounted on poster board. (Folding paper into thirds, as shown, also works.) Selected items should be those that illustrate why the book is a "must read." The oral presentation and poster board items can be generated as students answer three questions about the book. For more detailed information about designing book trailers, see *www.sblceastconn.org/notmegbooks2009.htm.*

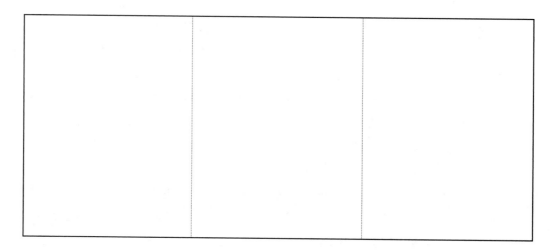

1 "Why did you like this book?"

2 "Why should a friend read it?"

3 "What was your favorite part and why?"

At the conclusion of their work, the students gather in small groups to share their book trailer displays and ideas about the book.

Q1—Why did you like this book?	Q2—Why should a friend read it?	Q3—What was your favorite part and why?

Intermediate Level

Using the same poster board idea used at the beginning level and working with a peer, students create an advertisement to sell a book previously read during independent reading. They are encouraged to write a song or a poem about a character in the story, using original questions or headings on the display board. Students present their boards to a small group and "sell" their books. Possible headings include the following:

Favorite Character	Poem/Song	Character Quotes/Thoughts
Description with details	Cinquains, acrostic, and haiku poems are great ways for students to share story elements involving the character	What did the character say/feel/think?

Advanced Level

Students use the same display board idea (used in the beginning and intermediate levels), changing the headings of the three columns. Each working with a peer, students create a song or rap about their book. They include a personal connection and a biography of the author. The Internet can help students research information about the author.

Rap Describing Book	Personal Connection	All About the Author
His name is Wilbur, a very smart pig He talks and walks, and dances a jig . . .	I am like Wilbur in a lot of ways because . . .	E. B. White has written *Stuart Little, The Trumpet of the Swan*

Tech It Out!

Students meet with their book buddies once a week to discuss what has recently been read. Book buddies can be pairs or groups of students in the same class or grade level or across grade levels. The teacher meets with teams of students to videotape their interactions as they engage in partner tutoring, share "book raps," or participate in a "book sale." Students can also do this more independently by using iPhoto. As the students watch the videos they discuss their oral performances by thinking about questions such as

"Did I speak loudly enough?"

"Did I speak slowly enough to be understood?"

"Did I present enough information to 'sell' my book?"

"Did my personal connections help the listener understand more about the characters and me?"

For additional ideas, visit *www.olemiss.k12.in.us/intervention/behavior/peerreport. pdf.*

Suggested Websites and Books

www.leeandlow.com
www.glencoe.com/sec/teachingtoday
istudy.psu.edu/FirstYearModules/PeerTutoring/PeerTutorInfo.htm

Campbell, Rod—*Dear Zoo: A Lift-the-Flap Book* (2005); Little Simon.
Ellis, Deborah—*Three Wishes: Palestinian and Israeli Children Speak* (2006); Groundwood Books.
Monk, Isabell—*Hope* (2004); First Avenue Editions.
Ravel, Edeet—*The Saver* (2010); Groundwood Books.
Smith, Sherri—*Hot, Sour, Salty, Sweet* (2009); Laurel Leaf.

References

Bauer, E. B., Manyak, P. C., & Cook, C. (2010). Supporting content learning for English learners. *The Reading Teacher, 63*(5), 430–432.

Ogle, D., & Correa-Kovtun, A. (2010). Supporting English-language learners and struggling readers in content literacy with the "partner reading and content, too" routine. *The Reading Teacher, 63*(7), 532–542.

Van Keer, H., & Vanderlinde, R. (2010). The impact of cross-age peer tutoring on third and sixth graders' reading awareness strategy use and reading comprehension. *Middle Grades Research Journal, 5*(1), 33–45.

Peer Tutoring Guide

Course: _____ Teacher: _____ Date: _____

Tutor: _____ Partner: _____

Goal: _____

_____

_____

Pages to Read: _____

After Reading:

1. What I don't understand (e.g., words, a main idea, a process): _____

_____

_____

_____

2. What my partner explained: _____

_____

_____

_____

_____

3. Three examples of what we practiced: _____

   a. _____

_____

   b. _____

_____

   c. _____

_____

4. What I now better understand: _____

_____

_____

5. Attached are my completed products: _____

_____

_____

Reading Comprehension Strategy Guide

Common Core Standard

Use context to confirm or self-correct word recognition and understanding, rereading as necessary.

TESOL Standard

Use an array of strategies with visually supported text with a partner to infer meaning.

Focus skill: Comprehension
Secondary skill: Vocabulary/
Conversing about Texts

What Is the Purpose?

Apply and understand comprehension strategies used while reading a text.

What Is the Research Base?

Reading comprehension involves the ability to read selectively and to glean important information from a text (Appleman, 2010; Ellery, 2010; Lapp, Fisher, & Johnson, 2010). *My Reading Comprehension Strategy Guide* (Work Page 19.1) provides a resource students can use to monitor and record their efforts to derive meanings from their readings. Becoming metacognitively aware can help students make transparent their bundled use of effective reading strategies .

Teacher Modeling and Guiding

1 The teacher displays Work Page 19.1, My Reading Comprehension Strategy Guide, on the document camera for all students to see.

2 This guide works well when students are looking at text such as chapters from a textbook.

3 Before the students begin to read, the teacher shows them how to fill in the top of the Strategy Guide by filling in the title and page numbers of the passage being read.

4 Next, the teacher reads aloud the passage that has been displayed on the document camera. While reading the teacher thinks aloud about what strategies are being used.

5 For example, the teacher might say, "Let's see. I am looking at this Comprehension Strategy Guide, and I see the words *skim, scan*. I know that means to look quickly at headings, subheadings, and vocabulary words that will help me get an idea of what this passage is about. So let me do that now. I will write exactly what I did. I read the title section and I scanned the passage for new vocabulary words."

6 The teacher then shows students how to fill in the Strategy Guide. (See Example 19.1.)

7 The teacher may complete this lesson over an extended time period by modeling a single strategy and then inviting students to practice in pairs. Although strategies are modeled individually, it is important to explain to the students that they use their strategies together, not one at a time.

8 The teacher guides students as they use comprehension strategies to make explicit their thinking. The teacher may tell students that "if you skim, reread, slow your pace, and try to react to what you read, you can derive more meaning as you read."

Peer Collaboration and Extension

1 During this time, students work in heterogeneous partner teams to complete Work Page 19.1.

2 As they work, the teacher moves among the students offering cues and prompts and asking questions that support their performance. The teacher may use prompts such as "Take a look at these strategies. Which ones are you using or did you use after you read this passage? Do you know exactly when you might have used these strategies? Was it while you were reading paragraph 1? Paragraph 2?" The teacher

Text and Pages I Read: <u>United States</u>: Adventures in Time and Place

<u>Spanish Missions, page 256</u>

A Strategy I Used	An Example (ideas, words)
Skim, scan	After reading the title section, I scanned the passage for new vocabulary words.
Slow pace for relevant or important information	Paragraph 1: I reread the second paragraph because I wanted to be reminded of the dates Coronado explored the Southwest.
Make and monitor predictions	Paragraph 2: I predicted that the author would discuss how the Spanish traveled and lived in Mexico and in South America.
Notice familiar ideas	I have visited some missions in California and I remembered the architecture and the peaceful atmosphere of the missions.
Interpret meanings	Paragraph 2: Because the first settlement was named for St. Augustine, he must have been an important person to the Spanish people.
Evaluate sensibility of ideas	Because of the existence of gold in the Southwest, it makes sense that the Spanish traveled into this area.
Form personal opinions	I think that our current society still enjoys many of the contributions brought by the Spanish from Spain (food, architecture, language, religion)
Reread important information	Paragraph 3: I reread the section about St. Augustine's location because I wanted to determine its specific location in Florida.
Summarize text, restate important ideas	Spanish explorers came to the North American continent before the English had formed the 13 colonies. They benefitted as well as contributed.
Classmate's/teacher's ideas that affected my ideas	After discussing Spain's arrival to the Americas, I realized that many areas of the Atlantic coast were settled before the English arrived in Jamestown.

EXAMPLE 19.1. Completed Work Page 19.1.

also makes note of the similar needs existing among the students. This information will help him or her to offer later interventions to students with similar needs.

Teacher Differentiating and Accommodating

From the information the teacher gained as students worked collaboratively, he or she is now able to offer instruction similar to the examples that follow that provide guided interventions to students with similar needs. As the teacher does so, the others can read texts similar to those listed as suggested books or can be engaged with the Tech It Out! activity. They can also continue having text-supported discussions that are supported by information they noted on the Strategy Guide.

Beginning Level

The teacher reads aloud an informational text, pausing after each page/section to give students a chance to write on three different colored sticky notes what they *think* (yellow), *wonder* (blue), and *learned* (green). Students place their ideas (sticky notes) on a "Wonder Wheel" chart in the appropriate sections. The teacher shares all ideas with the class at the conclusion of the read-aloud and continues with a conversation on the reading/topic, using students' ideas to support their comprehension. Students talk in pairs about their ideas, posing new questions and talking about new information learned.

Intermediate Level

After a shared reading lesson using an informational text, students are grouped in triads. One student becomes the *thinker,* one student the *wonderer,* and one student the *learner.* By assuming these roles students can practice verbalizing what is going on in their minds. Students help one another by answering questions and thinking and wondering together. They return to the text to support their thinking and conversation.

Advanced Level

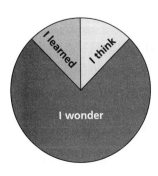

Students can make their own Wonder Wheels by taking three different colored circles, making one cut into the center of each circle, and fitting them together so they overlap completely to make a pie chart. Students write their thoughts (I think), wonderings (I wonder), and what they learned (I learned) on the different sections of the wheel. The Wonder Wheel pictured here shows that this student has many wonderings and fewer ideas in her "I think" and "I learned" sections after reading an informational text. Students can base their answers on metacognitive strategies. For example, one student may write, "I think that I mostly form personal opinions about what I read. I learned that I need to become better at interpreting meanings from what I read. I wonder a lot about how to evaluate the sensibility of ideas."

Tech It Out!

Groups of students use a microphone and digital video camera to film themselves making an infomercial or public service announcement about a text they have read. The teacher reminds students that an infomercial is typically several minutes in length and serves to "sell" a product, whereas a public service announcement is brief and serves to influence and inform viewers. He or she also tells them that they must not wander from the story or the facts. Their presentation must be true to what is said in the text. The teacher establishes guidelines for either format (or both) for students. Students can view one another's videos and provide feedback, if desired. Check out *mx.nthu.edu.tw/~katchen/professional/Using%20the%20video%20 camera.htm* for other ways to use a video camera in the classroom, including role playing and oral presentations.

Suggested Websites and Books

www.readwritethink.org/classroom-resources/lesson-plans/scaffolding-comprehension-
   strategies-using-95.html
www.youtube.com/watch?v=CCHspWIOFE8
www.readinglady.com/ . . . /Inferring%20lesson%20plan-grade%203%20from%20Elouise.pdf

Bolden, Tonya—*Portraits of African-American Heroes* (2005); Puffin.
Degen, Bruce—*Jamberry* (1985); HarperCollins.
Kimmel, Eric A.—*The Magic Dreidels; A Hanukkah Story* (1997); Holiday House.
Palacios, Argentina—*Standing Tall: The Stories of Ten Hispanic Americans* (1994); Scholastic.
Zlata, Filipovic—*Zlata's Diary: A Child's Life in Sarajevo* (2006); Penguin.

References

Appleman, D. (2010). *Adolescent literacy and the teaching of reading: Lessons for teachers of literature*. Urbana, IL: National Council of Teachers of English.

Ellery, V. (2010). How do we teach reading as a strategic, decision-making process? *The Reading Teacher, 63*(5), 434–436.

Lapp, D., Fisher, D., & Johnson, K. (2010). Text mapping plus: Improving comprehension through supported retellings. *Journal of Adolescent and Adult Literacy, 53*(5), 423–426.

My Reading Comprehension Strategy Guide

Name: _____

Text and Pages I Read: _____

_____

A Strategy I Used	An Example (ideas, words)
Skim, scan	
Slow pace for relevant or important information	
Make and monitor predictions	
Notice familiar ideas	
Interpret meanings	
Evaluate sensibility of ideas	
Form personal opinions	
Reread important information	
Summarize text, restate important ideas	
Classmate's/teacher's ideas that affected my ideas	

Read, Record, Report

Common Core Standard

With guidance and support, produce writing in which the development and organization are appropriate to task and purpose.

TESOL Standard

Self-assess drafts and produce final products using rubrics, guides, or other resources.

Focus skill: Pronunciation
Secondary skill: Vocabulary for Writing and Speaking

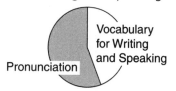

What Is the Purpose?

Use information gained from text to write topically connected text.

What Is the Research Base?

Writing proficiency is a "consequence of not only the time spent on the task, but also on the significance of the task and the quality of the instruction" (Lapp, Flood, Moore, & Nichols, 2005). Collaborative writing, particularly for English learners, invites all students to contribute ideas through verbal input shared during brainstorming and planning (Nelson, 2008). *Read, Record, Report* is an integrated, collaborative postreading activity that supports students' writing and comprehension as they reread and discuss, write notes, and develop a summary statement about what they have read.

Teacher Modeling and Guiding

1 The teacher begins by showing the students a copy of Work Page 20.1, Teacher Dictation, Our Questions.

2 The teacher reads aloud from the text or from a summary/synopsis of a previously read text compiled by the teacher and the students.

3 As the teacher reads, the students write the sentences they hear. The teacher should read slowly enough so students can record as much of each sentence as possible. (Note: It is okay if students do not get each word dictated by the teacher.)

4 If students are unsure of a word, they should first attempt to write it and then leave a space for the unknown word. If this is too difficult, they should put the first letter followed by a dash for every word they hear.

5 The teacher models this process for the students and thinks aloud about the dictation and the writing process. "I heard the teacher say that by 1440 Tenochititlan was the capital of the mighty Aztec empire. So I will write that sentence here where it says 'Teacher Dictation.'" (See Example 20.1.)

6 After dictating the sentences to the students, the teacher models how students will ask each other questions using the words *who, what, where, when, why,* and

---

Teacher Dictation

Student Name: _Tenochititlan was the capital of the mighty Aztec empire._

_____

_____

_____

_____

_____

Our Questions

1. _Where is Tenochititlan?_

_____

2. _____

_____

3. _____

_____

EXAMPLE 20.1. Completed Work Page 20.1.

how (five *W*'s + *H*). "So I see that I wrote that Tenochititlan was the capital of the Aztec empire. I am going to ask a question using the word *what*. What was the capital of the Aztec empire?"

7 The teacher continues modeling these questions using the five *W*'s + *H* and the dictated sentences. (Note: *Who, what, where, when, why,* and *how* posters can be displayed at the front of the class for easy reference.)

8 After the teacher has modeled a question, he or she invites students to respond. This can be done in the form of a friendly competition as teams compete to answer each other's questions.

Peer Collaboration and Extension

1 During this time, students work in heterogeneous groups.

2 After writing the dictated sentences the teacher read aloud, students work in groups to come up with questions to try to "stump" one another.

3 As they work, the teacher moves among the students, offering cues and prompts and asking questions that support their performance. The teacher also makes note of the similar needs existing among the students. This information can help the teacher to offer later interventions to students with similar needs. "I see you have a sentence here about what I read out loud. Can you think of a question you can ask about this topic? Refer to the five *W*'s + *H* (*who, what, where, when, why,* and *how*) posters to help you think of questions."

Teacher Differentiating and Accommodating

Beginning Level

The teacher reads aloud an informational text, such as Sally Lucas's *Road to Reading: Dancing Dinos*, which is appropriate for students at the beginning level. After the read-aloud, the teacher gives the students an opening statement such as "Dinosaurs are very interesting." In pairs, students orally make a list of three or four facts they learned from the read-aloud. On chart paper, the teacher has prepared the opening sentence to a paragraph about the information/topic being studied. The students are asked, one at a time, to add to the paragraph with the facts they listed, being careful not to repeat a fact. The teacher records the facts, developing a class-created paragraph. Students read the text multiple times after each fact is added. Names can be added after each fact so that the students "own" the text. Students continue to use the five *W*'s + *H* chart developed in the earlier whole-class lesson.

Dinosaurs are very interesting. Some dinosaurs ate meat. (Dalyasia) Dinosaurs are extinct. (Steven) Some dinosaurs were herbivores. (Ali) The biggest dinosaur was a Brachiosaurus. (Ricky)

Intermediate Level

The teacher reads aloud an informational text at the intermediate level, such as Lucille Davis's *Cesar Chavez*. In small groups, the students write a list of facts they learned while listening. The facts are then used to create a paragraph with a prepared opening sentence that was decided upon together. The paragraph is written as each student in the group writes one of his or her facts. The process occurs as one member writes a sentence then passes the paper to the next member until each member has added a sentence and the paragraph is completed. Facts cannot be repeated. Cohesive paragraphs can have three or four different handwriting styles and three or four different facts. Students can use the five *W*'s + *H* chart for reference and support.

Advanced Level

Students are orally given an opening question or statement; the teacher then reads aloud an informational text, such as Robert Nicholson and Claire Watts's *The Aztecs: Journey into Civilization* (e.g., "What caused the downfall of the great Aztec people under the leadership of Montezuma II?"—*The Aztec nation was powerful until a series of disastrous mistakes caused its downfall.*) The students write this opening question or statement on their own papers. As the teacher reads the text, the students add facts to answer the question or expand the statement. The teacher pauses at predetermined places in the text, allowing the students to record their facts. The teacher rereads the selection, and the students write an informational paragraph using the facts they learned to support the opening sentence or to answer the question. Students reread their paragraphs each time a new fact is added as they improve their reading fluency and watch their paragraphs "grow."

Tech It Out!

After listening to a text read aloud or reading it independently, pairs of students generate a list of facts or vocabulary words relating to the topic being studied. These facts and/or words can be used to write questions using the five *W*'s + *H*. Using Puzzlemaker, students can create and customize word searches and crossword puzzles using their own word lists. For ideas on using Puzzlemaker in your classroom, check out *puzzlemaker.school.discovery.com* or *www.puzzle-maker.com/*CW.

Suggested Websites and Books

www.criticalreading.com/writing_reading.htm
www.english-4kids.com
www.readwritethink.org/classroom-resources/lesson-plans

Choi, Yangsook—*The Name Jar* (2006); Dragonfly Books.
King, Laurie—*Hear My Voice: A Multicultural Anthology of Literature from the United States* (1993); Dale Seymour.
Mazer, Anne—*America Street* (1993); Perfection Learning.
Nikola-Lisa, W.—*Bein' with You This Way* (1995); Lee & Low Books.
Rosen, Michael—*We're Going on a Bear Hunt* (2009); Margaret K. McElderry.

References

Lapp, D., Flood, J., Moore, K., & Nichols, M. (2005). *Teaching literacy in first grade.* New York: Guilford Press.

Nelson, N. (2008). The reading–writing nexus in discourse research. In C. Bazerman (Ed.), *Handbook of research on writing* (pp. 435–450). New York: Routledge.

Read, S. (2010). A model for scaffolding writing instruction: IMSCI. *The Reading Teacher, 64*(1), 47–52.

Teacher Dictation, Our Questions

Teacher Dictation

Student Name: _____

_____

_____

_____

_____

_____

_____

_____

_____

_____

_____

_____

_____

_____

_____

_____

_____

Our Questions

1. _____

_____

2. _____

_____

3. _____

_____

4. _____

_____

5. _____

_____

Making Connections

Common Core Standard

Cite several pieces of textual evidence to support analysis of what the text says explicitly as well as inferences and connections drawn from the text.

TESOL Standard

Connect information from text to oneself and personal experiences.

Focus skill: Comprehension
Secondary skill: Fluency in Language and Reading

Fluency in Language and Reading

Comprehension

What Is the Purpose?

Use text-based information to support analysis and inferences drawn from and among texts.

What Is the Research Base?

Teaching with a multicultural perspective helps students develop an appreciation and understanding of other cultures as well as their own. Books and meaningful instructional activities based on the countries, cultures, and life experiences of the students invites them to form personal connections with the stories and informational texts they read (Nikitina, 2010; Shatz & Wilkinson, 2010; Taliaferro, 2009). *Making Connections* provides students with pre-, during-, and postreading strategies to interact meaningfully with text-supported information and literature in multiple contexts.

Teacher Modeling and Guiding

1 The teacher begins with a prereading activity, developing questions related to the themes of a text. The questions should invite conversation from the students. These questions are written on chart paper are placed in the front of the room. Example 21.1 shows themes that could have been developed before reading *I Speak English for My Mom* by Muriel Stanek.

2 The teacher models the process by thinking aloud about the story themes/questions. In response to the first question in Example 21.1, the teacher may say, "Leave one school and enter a new school? Hmm. Yes, I have. I had to do that when I was 9 years old. My family had to move to California. We used to live in Ohio. I was sad to leave my hometown." As the teacher talks aloud for the students, he or she records the words on the chart for the students to see.

3 Next, the teacher invites students to talk in pairs about their experiences in moving to a new place or experiencing something for the first time (e.g., starting school, playing soccer, participating in a piano recital). As students talk in pairs, the teacher listens in to make sure they understand the question and can make con-

Story Themes/Questions	My Response	
1 Have you ever had to leave one school and enter a new school? (Enter the grade level.)	Ricardo—My family moved here from Texas when I was in the fourth grade.	Guillermo—I moved to San Diego and changed schools in the fourth grade.
2 Have you been in a situation where you did not understand the language being spoken?	Stephanie—I didn't understand the man in the grocery store when I was with my mom.	Erica—When I watch television, I do not understand the program.
3 Have you been in a place without a close friend?	Mario—When I go home on the bus I don't have any friends.	Elizabeth—In my first year here I didn't have friends.

EXAMPLE 21.1. Completed Work Page 21.1.

nections. If students struggle, the teacher guides them with prompts: "Think for a minute. In the book the characters felt a certain way. When have you felt that way? Tell me about that. Often we can make connections with characters and can feel the same way they feel."

4 After students have had a chance to talk in pairs, the teacher can act as a scribe for the students (or invite students to write for themselves). Student responses can be written on the whole-class chart.

5 The teacher now models for the students how to complete Work Page 21.1, Making Connections. An example might look like that shown as Example 21.1.

6 The teacher writes story themes/questions that come to mind and also shows students how to make connections that appear in the in the "My Response" column.

Peer Collaboration and Extension

1 During this time, students work in heterogeneous groups.

2 Students discuss potential questions and themes together that relate to a shared text or read-aloud. These can be questions or themes from a teacher read-aloud, book club text, or chapter from a textbook.

3 As students discuss ideas for the first column, the conversations should continue, discussing their responses for the second column. (See Example 21.1.)

4 As they work, the teacher moves among the students offering cues and prompts and asking questions that support their performance. "I see you wonder about the actions of the character in the book. You wonder why the protagonist would act that way. Think about someone you know who may also have acted that way. That's how you make connections. Think about what's happening in the book *and* how that relates to your own life." The teacher also makes note of the similar needs existing among the students. This information will help the teacher to offer later interventions to students with similar needs.

Teacher Differentiating and Accommodating

Beginning Level

In small groups, the students are given a problem posed as a question which is drawn from a suggested story or a text at the beginning level, such as Eve Bunting's *How Many Days to America?: A Thanksgiving Story*. As a group, the students think about how they would answer the questions posed by the problem. The teacher records the students' oral responses on chart paper, which are then reread by the class. The teacher can also have students work in small groups and think and talk about a problem question of their own that may occur and how they would solve it. By talking in small groups and with partners, the students have many opportunities to develop their oral language as related to a textual experience.

> **EXAMPLE**
>
> Would moving to a new home cause you to feel like the character? Please explain.

Intermediate Level

After reading a text at the intermediate level, such as Steven Kellogg's *Best Friends*, pairs of students are given a scenario using familiar characters. Staying true to the theme of the story, students develop the problem *and* the solution for the characters, recording their ideas to share with the class. Students can perform their scenarios in front of the class after rehearsing and rereading their written work.

> **EXAMPLE**
>
> My friend keeps telling lies. My solution is to talk to my friend and tell her that if she continues to lie, no one will believe or trust her when she tells the truth.

Advanced Level

After reading an advanced-level text, such as Pam Muñoz Ryan's *Esperanza Rising*, pairs of students work together to write and talk about a problem in the text. One student assumes the role of the character in the book and the other plays him- or herself. A dialogue between the two students may sound something like this:

STUDENT 1 [portraying Esperanza]: How did you deal with the loss of someone you love?

STUDENT 2: My Nana died last year and it was very difficult for me. I cried a lot and wrote down my feelings.

Students can record their ideas, rereading them often.

Tech It Out!

The teacher invites students to use the Internet or e-mail to contact and send a message to the author or illustrator of a shared text or another person who may have a connection to the text or topic (e.g., if the book is about baseball, students could write to a baseball player). Websites such as Scholastic (*www.scholastic.com*) provide links to authors' websites, which often invite visitors to contact the author. Similarly, if the text relates to concepts that lend themselves to e-mailing people in areas in which the student draws connections (e.g., businesses, farmers, the president, etc.), the teacher can invite students to construct and e-mail messages to make real-world connections. He or she might instead choose to have these written to a designated on-site adult, such as a parent volunteer, who then replies to the e-mail.

Suggested Websites and Books

www.colorincolorado.org/article/30104
manythings.org
adlit.org

Alexie, Sherman—*The Absolutely True Diary of a Part-Time Indian* (2009); Little, Brown Books for Young Readers.
Barton, Byron—*The Three Bears* (1991); HarperFestival.
Miller, J. Philip; & Greene, Sheppard M.—*We All Sing with the Same Voice* (2005); HarperCollins.
Soto, Gary—*Buried Onions* (2006); Graphia.
Stead, Rebecca—*When You Reach Me* (2009); Wendy Lamb Books.

References

Nikitina, L. (2010). Addressing pedagogical dilemmas in a constructivist language learning experience. *Journal of the Scholarship of Teaching and Learning, 10*(2), 90–106.

Shatz, M., & Wilkinson, L. C. (Eds.). (2010). *The education of English language learners: Research to practice.* New York: Guilford Press.

Taliaferro, C. (2009). Using picture books to expand adolescents' imaginings of themselves and others. *English Journal, 99*(2), 30–36.

Making Connections

Name: _____

Story Themes/Questions	My Response
1	
2	
3	
4	

My Conversation Log

Common Core Standard
Use information from texts in order to write or speak about a subject knowledgeably.

TESOL Standard
Respond to questions and statements according to audience or situation.

Focus skill: Pronunciation
Secondary skill: Comprehension

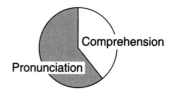

What Is the Purpose?

Pose text-based questions, offer answers, and think about supportive text information while participating in a whole-class discussion.

What Is the Research Base?

Focused conversational speaking provides ELLs opportunities to focus on grammatical tenses, to organize sentence structure, and to implement vocabulary through meaningful contexts (Grisham & Wolsey, 2006; Huang & Hung, 2010; Opitz & Harding-DeKam, 2007). *My Conversation Log* provides students an opportunity to practice reading, writing, listening, and speaking. The Conversation Log guides students through a process of anticipating, planning, and evaluating their thoughts while engaging in a communicative exchange.

Teacher Modeling and Guiding

1 The teacher begins by stating the purpose of the lesson. "The purpose for using the Conversation Log is to help you to participate in our whole-class conversation. The questions you write will help you to focus your thinking and support your talking with the whole class and me."

2 Before reading, the teacher models how to fill out the top part and items 1 and 2 of Work Page 22.1.

3 The teacher models the main topic or theme of the text being read. The page numbers are also recorded on the Work Page. To illustrate, the teacher models Example 22.1.

Name: _____ Date: _____

1. **Topic/Title:** <u>Animals living in the Arctic region.</u>
_____

2. **Preparation: Pages to Read:** <u>Pages 1 and 2 of the article "Coastlands of the Arctic."</u>
_____

3. **My Discussion Question:** <u>How do animals live in the Arctic?</u>
_____

4. **Answer to My Question:** <u>Many seabirds, ducks, walruses, and seals feed at sea. These</u>
<u>animals come ashore or onto the coastal ice to rest. Polar bears wander between land</u>
<u>and ice, to hunt and rest.</u>

5. **My Thoughts:** <u>More animals live in the Arctic region than I thought. I think I would like</u>
<u>to visit the Arctic region. The animals are beautiful and the environment is very different</u>
<u>from our own.</u>

6. **My During-Discussion Questions:** <u>How many years do polar bears live? Do penguins live</u>
<u>in the Arctic also? What do seals eat?</u>
_____

7. **What I understood:** <u>I understood Carlos when he explained that seal pups are born</u>
<u>white, and that when seals are under water they close their nostrils to keep the water</u>
<u>out.</u>
_____

EXAMPLE 22.1. Completed Work Page 22.1.

4 Then the teacher reads aloud the passage and models how to develop a question the students may like to ask during a whole-class discussion (Example 22.1, item 3).

5 Then, after orally reading the passage, the teacher models for students how to ask the question to the whole class. "I'm wondering how animals live in the Artic"? The teacher models for students how to record the answer a classmate provides (Example 22.1, item 4).

6 The teacher continues modeling for students how to complete items 5, 6, and 7 on Work Page 22.1 as they listen to the questions and answers posed by class members, recording their thoughts, their own additional questions, and important facts.

Peer Collaboration and Extension

1 During this time, students will work in heterogeneous groups or partner teams.

2 Students read a shared text such as a newspaper article, a *Weekly Reader*, or a passage from a textbook.

3 As they read, they fill in items 1, 2, and 3 on Work Page 22.1.

4 Once all students have completed the first three items, they pose questions and answers to their partners or team members, which help them to complete items 5, 6, and 7.

5 As they work, the teacher moves among the students offering cues and prompts and asking questions that support their performance. For example, he or she might say to a student who is unsure of the process, "The question you wrote here will be answered by a classmate. After your question is answered, you will have more thoughts and questions. The process of reading involves a lot of questioning, answering, and thinking." The teacher also makes note of the similar needs existing among the students. This information will help him or her to offer later interventions to those with similar needs.

Teacher Differentiating and Accommodating

From the information the teacher gained as students worked collaboratively, he or she is now able to offer instruction that provides guided interventions to students with similar needs. As the teacher does so, the others can read texts similar to those listed as suggested books, continue to work or share with a partner the Conversation Log, or engage with the Tech It Out! activity.

Beginning Level

The teacher asks students to have a conversation (in partners) about a content topic or a beginning-level book that was read aloud, such as *Wolves and Wild Dogs* by Christine Gunzi. Key topic/content vocabulary may be reviewed before the conversation to support students with ideas/language needed to compose their conversations. Each pair of students dictate their conversation, word for word, to the teacher. The teacher records the conversation on chart paper. When the conversation has been recorded, the students read it back to each other so illustrations can be added. Students can then share their conversations with other partners.

EXAMPLE: Vocabulary Reviewed after Read-Aloud

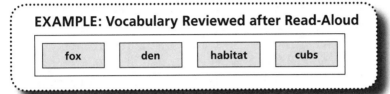

| fox | den | habitat | cubs |

EXAMPLE: Conversation

STUDENT 1: A fox's den is called an *earth*.

STUDENT 2: The female fox takes care of her cubs while they play.

Intermediate Level

Following a read-aloud from a fictional (E. B. White's *Charlotte's Web*) or informational text (*The Curse of King Tut's Tomb* by Michael Burgan), pairs of students orally share their reflections. As students question each other about the topic, plot, and characters, they record key words, phrases, and sentences in their conversation logs. They can also add illustrations. This activity ends with a class performance or sharing time.

Example: Conversation

STUDENT 1: Why do you think Charlotte is so smart? She knows everything!

STUDENT 2: I think Charlotte is so smart because she is a good listener.

Advanced Level

After a classroom read-aloud of a fictional (Scott O'Dell's *Island of the Blue Dolphins*) or informational (Kathleen Krull's *Lives of the Musicians*) text, students—in partners or small groups—assume the roles of the characters and then record a conversation related to the topic. Key vocabulary is reviewed and incorporated in the conversation. Students use this conversation as a Reader's Theatre script, practicing correct grammar and fluency. Students practice and present their offering to the class.

Tech It Out!

The teacher starts a threaded on-line discussion related to a particular topic among students in which he or she sends a blog or an e-mail message to a class-specific list-serv that includes all of the students (*www.mxcc.commnet.edu/distance/orientation/wdisc.html*). The message invites responses about the text read (or being read), and the replies by students are shared with all students on the listserv. As students read replies in their e-mails, they join the conversation and respond to each other as if in a written conversation. The subject line should remain the same for this threaded discussion and should relate to the text. When the teacher wants to start another threaded discussion about another text, he or she changes the subject line and proceeds with another threaded discussion about the new text. Each threaded discussion can remain in the teacher's blog or e-mail and students' e-mail for future reference/use. A school technology coordinator can help the teacher create e-mail accounts and a listserv for the students. For ideas and suggestions on how to teach the use of e-mail to students, check out *www.abcteach.com/directory/reading_comprehension.*

Suggested Websites and Books

inspiration.com/englishlanguagelearners
www.nwp.org/cs/public/print/resource/922
www.ehow.com/how_4464065_teach-writing-esl-students.html

Applegate, Katherine—*Home of the Brave* (2008); Square Fish.
Blohm, Judith; & Lapinsky, Terri—*Kids Like Me* (2006); Intercultural Press.
Bunting, Eve—*A Day's Work* (1997); Sandpiper.
Lowry, Lois—*Number the Stars* (1996); Laurel Leaf.
Taback, Simms—*Where Is My Friend?* (2006); Blue Apple Books.

References

Grisham, D. L., & Wolsey, T. D. (2006). Recentering the middle school classroom as a vibrant learning community: Students, literacy, and technology intersect. *Journal of Adolescent and Adult Literacy, 49*(8), 648–660.

Huang, H. D., & Hung, S. A. (2010). Examining the practice of a reading-to-speak test task: Anxiety and experience of EFL (English as a foreign language) students. *Asia Pacific Education Review, 11*(2), 235–242.

Opitz, M. F., & Harding-DeKam, J. L. (2007). Understanding and teaching English-language learners, *The Reading Teacher, 60*(6), 590–593.

My Conversation Log

Name: _____ Date: _____

1. Topic/Title: _____

_____

2. Preparation: Pages to Read: _____

_____

3. My Discussion Question: _____

_____

_____

_____

4. Answer to My Question: _____

_____

_____

_____

5. My Thoughts: _____

_____

_____

_____

6. My During-Discussion Questions: _____

_____

_____

_____

_____

7. What I Understood: _____

_____

_____

_____

_____

_____

Character Analysis

Common Core Standard

Describe characters in a story (e.g., their traits, motivations, or feelings) and explain how their actions contribute to the sequence of events.

TESOL Standard

Explain differences in character traits or points of view in characters portrayed in fiction.

Focus skill: Fluency
Secondary skill: Comprehension

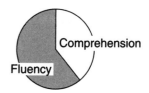

What Is the Purpose?

Use details from a text to support character analysis.

What Is the Research Base?

Analyzing elements of literature, such as character, plot, and theme, provides ELLs a purposeful context through which they can negotiate meaning (Appleman, 2009; Morgan & Hani, 2009; Ogle & Correa-Kovtun, 2010). Oral discussion offers ELLs a vehicle to contrast character traits, actions, and intentions. The *Character Analysis* activity provides a format for expanded analysis and interpretation of a character's motivation and traits.

Teacher Modeling and Guiding

1 After reading a text aloud, the teacher models for students how to think about or analyze and compare the characters. When doing so, he or she identifies actions, traits, and logical motivations. For example, the teacher might say, "Let's see. I'm thinking about Esperanza from *The House on Mango Street* by Sandra Cisneros, and I know that she is friendly, optimistic, and perseverant. She really knows what she wants. I will add those traits here." The teacher models where to record this information in Section A of Work Page 23.1, Character Analysis. Example 23.1 shows a filled-in version.

Book Title: House on Mango Street
Author: Sandra Cisneros

Character 1: Esperanza	**Character 2:** Ruthie
A. Three traits this character demonstrated are:	**A. Three traits this character demonstrated are:**
1. friendly	1. indecisiveness
2. optimistic	2. complimentary
3. perseverant	3. disenchanted
B. Three motivational factors I identified are:	**B. Three motivational factors I identified are:**
1. She hopes for a spacious house in a suburban neighborhood.	1. Ruthie can't decide if she wants to play Bingo. She had job offers but never accepted them.
2. Esperanza says, "One day I will pack my bags of books and paper. One day I will say good-bye to Mango. I am too strong for her to keep me here forever."	2. Ruthie enjoys the company of the neighborhood children.
3. Sandra Cisneros became a teacher and wrote about her struggles.	3. She cannot work to support herself.

C. How are these characters similar? Esperanza and Ruthie both enjoy the pleasure of social interaction and the beauty of nature.

D. How are these characters different? Esperanza hopes to escape from the life on Mango Street, whereas Ruthie is satisfied living there with her mother.

E. With whom can you associate one of these characters and their motives (e.g., a character in another book, a famous person, a historical figure, a family member, a friend)? Explain your response. I would associate Esperanza with myself because I am also a persevering, independent person.

EXAMPLE 23.1. Completed Work Page 23.1.

2 The teacher continues as Sections B, C, D , and E are modeled for students. The teacher may ask students to talk in pairs about the different sections of Work Page 23.1. As students talk, the teacher listens in to the conversations and redirects and prompts students as needed. She might say, "Think about the kind of character we are reading about. How would you describe Esperanza to someone who hasn't read the book?"

3 While the teacher models how to think about the different sections of Work Page 23.1, he or she invites students to think, pair, and share responses. As students respond, the teacher records their ideas.

4 Next the teacher invites a comparison of characters by saying, "Now I want you to think about Ruthie, another character in the same story. Work with a partner to complete the second column of the Character Analysis chart." While students talk in pairs, discussing their ideas, the teacher listens in, guiding and prompting as needed—for example, for students struggling with deciding which character shares similar qualities with them, "Talk about your qualities first and then decide if you are more like Esperanza or Ruthie."

Peer Collaboration and Extension

1 During this time, students work in heterogeneous groups or as partners.

2 Students use a selection from their independent reading book as their text when completing Work Page 23.1.

3 Students talk about character traits, motivational factors, and the similarities and differences. Students are encouraged to share all information about their characters with their groups.

4 One of the goals of this collaborative group work is to make sure students become familiar with characters, not only from their own texts, but also from their peers' texts.

5 The teacher should save time at the end of this lesson for sharing information about the students' characters.

6 As they work, the teacher moves among the students, offering cues and prompts and asking questions that support their performance. "You are writing about the characters' traits right here. Share this with a partner in your group. What do you notice?"

7 The teacher also makes note of the similar needs existing among the students. This information will help him or her to offer later interventions to students with similar needs.

Teacher Differentiating and Accommodating

Beginning Level

After reading a fictional text, such as a fairy tale, the students talk about the qualities of the characters. The teacher creates a chart of key characters. The teacher then leads a discussion and records the students' ideas that illustrate the qualities of each character.

Characters	Good	Reason	Evil	Reason
Snow White	X	She is kindhearted and cheerful. She takes care of the dwarfs.		
Wicked Witch			X	She is selfish and she wants Snow White dead.
Doc	X	He is reliable and the leader of the dwarfs.		
Prince	X	He is hopeful and he loves Snow White.		
Woodsman	X	He is brave and he won't kill Snow White.		

Intermediate Level

Using a report card form created by the teacher on chart paper, the students work in partners or small groups to grade the behaviors of each character. This occurs after the teacher shares a narrative text at the intermediate level, such as *Snow White and the Seven Dwarfs*. The students choose two or three characters to compare. Categories are established by the teacher and/or students. Students record the grades and reasons to support each grade given.

Characters	Evil	Selfish	Thoughtful	Honest
Snow White	F—She is not evil at all; she is kind and caring.	C—She takes over the dwarfs' home.	B+—She wants to take care of the dwarfs.	A—She believes the Wicked Witch's story is truthful.
Wicked Witch	A+—she wants to kill Snow White.	A—She wants to be the fairest in all the land.	D—She wanted to share an apple with Snow White.	F—She lied to Snow White and the dwarfs.

Advanced Level

Students choose a character from their independent reading and talk about what the character might need to do to improve his or her grade. For example, after reading *The Recess Queen* by Alexis O'Neill, a student may choose to become the character Mean Jean. The student may tell his or her classmates that although he or she received a C– in friendliness, he or she was going to work hard to improve that grade to a B+. The student would do things like share recess equipment, not push peers in line, hold doors open for others, and so on. This is a great way for students to talk about characters and understand their attributes and qualities. A great website to help students write resumes for characters in historical fiction is *www.readwritething.org/lessons/lesson_view.aspi?d=295.*

Tech It Out!

Using Inspiration software or the draw functions in Microsoft Word, or another integrated program, the teacher encourages students to create or use graphic organizers to develop character websites to define the characteristics, thoughts, and actions of characters in the text. These can be kept in a digital portfolio on the computer or printed out to display in class. Another way the teacher can help students analyze characters in their reading is to teach them how to create a résumé using a word processing program on the computer. Many versions of Microsoft Word feature a wizard that leads users through the steps needed to create a résumé . The teacher asks students to select a character from the text and create a résumé for that character. The teacher prints these out and uses them with students to analyze their contributions to the story. To find more ways to use a digital camera in the classroom, the teacher can check out *www.hardin.k12.ky.us/res_techn/tec/digital camera/primary.htm.*

Suggested Websites and Books

www.educationalrap.com/song/characters-setting-plot.html
www.teach-nology.com/worksheets/graphic
www2.scholastic.com/browse/unitplan.jsp?id=18

Amery, Heather—*Stories from around the World* (2010) Usborne Books.
Crew, Linda—*Children of the River* (1991); Laurel Leaf.
Lewis, Kevin—*Chugga-Chugga Choo-Choo* (1999); Hyperion Books.
McDonough, Yona Zeldis—*Who Was Harriet Tubman?* (2002); Grosset & Dunlap.
Staples, Suzanne Fisher—*Shabanu, Daughter of the Wind* (2003); Laurel Leaf.

References

Appleman, D. (2009). *Critical encounters in high school English: Teaching literary theory to adolescents* (2nd ed.). New York: Teachers College Press.

Morgan, H., & York, K. C. (2009). Examining multiple perspectives with creative think-alouds. *The Reading Teacher, 63*(4), 307–311.

Ogle, D., & Correa-Kovtun, A. (2010). Supporting English-language learners and struggling readers in content literacy with the "partner reading and content, too" routine. *The Reading Teacher, 63*(7), 532–542.

Character Analysis

Name: _____

Book Title: _____

Author: _____
_____

Character 1:	Character 2:
A. Three traits this character demonstrated are:	**A. Three traits this character demonstrated are:**
1. _____	1. _____
2. _____	2. _____
3. _____	3. _____
B. Three motivational factors I identified are:	**B. Three motivational factors I identified are:**
1. _____ _____ _____	1. _____ _____ _____
2. _____ _____ _____	2. _____ _____ _____
3. _____ _____ _____	3. _____ _____ _____

C. How are these characters similar? _____
_____

D. How are these characters different? _____
_____

E. With whom can you associate one of these characters and their motives (e.g., a character in another book, a famous person, a historical figure, a family member, a friend)? Explain your response. _____
_____
_____

Explain: How do the interactions between the main and subordinate characters in this story affect the plot? Do the interactions result in main events that help formulate the plot? What are they?

Interview/Conversation with a Character

Common Core Standard

Acknowledge differences in the points of view of characters, such as by speaking in a different voice for each character when reading dialogue aloud.

TESOL Standard

Compare–contrast character traits or points of view of characters in fiction.

Focus skill: Comprehension
Secondary skill: Fluency

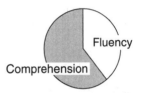

What Is the Purpose?

Understand, explain, and add support for a fictional character's perspective.

What Is the Research Base?

Guiding ELLs through literary analysis provides a context for augmenting their reading comprehension, reinforcing concepts through repetition and scaffolding analytical processes (Justice & Sofka, 2010; McLaughlin, 2010; Melin, 2010). *Interview/Conversation with a Character* provides students an opportunity to analyze a character's actions and to reflect on a character's motivations. This communicative activity can be used to discuss the actions and motivations of historical or current figures in society or can become a platform where two characters from different books converse with one another.

Teacher Modeling and Guiding

1 The teacher directs students to select one fictional or historical character from a book or story whom they would like to interview. He or she uses Example 24.1 to model how one student, as the interviewee, will answer questions posed by the interviewer. "So, if I were Cinderella I would say ... let's see ... I think the most significant task I have accomplished is getting along with my stepsisters. Yes, I have worked very hard at that. Notice the tone as well as the words I am using to show my point of view. As I think about how mean her sisters were to Cinderella, I agree that she has tried hard to get along with them."

2 The teacher models for students a few more responses that the character (in this case, Cinderella) may give. Be sure to continue to illustrate how these glimpses into her character help us to understand her perspective or point of view. For example, when looking at question 3 the teacher might say, "Cinderella believes in forgiveness, as shown when she says, 'I would tell my stepmother and stepsisters that I forgive their selfish actions.'"

3 The teacher invites pairs of students to use given questions in Example 24.1 to come up with text-supported responses.

4 Once students understand the given questions and have taken turns at answering them from the perspective of the character, the teacher asks them to work collaboratively to complete the Cinderella example or to select a new book/character and complete Work Page 24.1.

Peer Collaboration and Extension

1 During this time, students work as heterogeneous partners or groups.

2 In small groups, students complete Work Page 24.1, Interview/Conversation with a Character.

3 Because students are working collaboratively, they should choose one text but each select a different character from that text. For example, if they choose *Charlotte's Web* by E. B. White, the students in the group could assume the roles of Charlotte, Fern, Wilbur, and Templeton.

4 Each student fills out Work Page 24.1 and then practices the interviewing process. After all groups have had time to prepare interview questions and responses, they perform their interviews (much like a talk show panel) in front of the class. The rest of the class guesses what book the characters are from.

5 As they work, the teacher moves among the students, offering cues and prompts and asking questions that support their performance. For example, to a student

Conversation with <u>Cinderella</u>
(Character)

Book Title: <u>Cinderella</u>

Author: <u>Disney</u>

1. **What is the most important task you have accomplished?** <u>The most important task I have accomplished is getting along with my stepsisters.</u>

   Why do you consider this accomplishment the most important? <u>I consider this task the most important because I was able to show them how to be patient and loving even when our deeds are not appreciated.</u>

2. **In your opinion, what was the biggest problem you encountered, and how did you solve it** <u>The biggest problem I encountered was living with a stepmother who favored her own daughters. I solved the problem by focusing on my hopes and dreams.</u>

3. **What would you like to say to another character in this story or event?** <u>I would tell my stepmother and stepsisters that I forgive their selfish actions.</u>

4. **What was the greatest personal motivation in your life?** <u>I wanted to demonstrate a loving attitude to the insensitive people in my life.</u>

5. **If you could change one thing about your life or the outcome of the story, or an event, what would it be?** <u>I would ask my father, stepmother, and stepsisters to live with me in the palace.</u>

6. **What did you enjoy most during the events of this story?** <u>I enjoyed dancing with the prince at the ball.</u>

7. **What was the funniest or most unexpected event you experienced?** <u>The most unexpected event I experienced was when my fairy godmother visited me and helped me prepare for the ball.</u>

8. **Who was the greatest support to you? Why? How?** <u>My fairy godmother was the greatest support to me because she understood my hopes and helped me find happiness in my life. Most of all, she loved me.</u>

9. **What effect did this support have in your life?** <u>My fairy godmother gave me the courage to follow my dream.</u>

10. **What behavior of another character surprised, disappointed, or pleased you? Why?** <u>I was very pleased to see that the prince was looking for me after the ball. I didn't think I would ever see him again.</u>

11. **What worried or concerned you most?** <u>I was worried that I wouldn't see the prince again.</u>

12. **What was an obstacle you encountered and how can you learn from your experience?** <u>I wanted to go to the ball. I think that perseverance and keeping a positive attitude can provide happiness in life.</u>

13. **Could your obstacle have been prevented? How?** <u>My stepmother could have invited me to go with her and my stepsisters to the ball.</u>

14. **What do you now hope for yourself or for someone else?** <u>I hope that my stepsisters' dreams come true.</u>

15. **What advice would you now give to use?** <u>I would tell people to be patient as they wait for their dreams to come true.</u>

EXAMPLE 24.1. Completed Work Page 24.1.

stumped about answering question 8 about Templeton, the teacher might say, "Think about the times Templeton helped Charlotte and Wilbur. Did he help them because he was basically kind or because he was being given something in return?" This question alerts the student to think about the underlying motivation of the character. The teacher may need to further point out that this behavior could be considered a disappointing character trait or perspective of friendship. During this time the teacher also makes note of the similar needs existing among the students. This information can help him or her to offer later interventions to students with similar needs.

Teacher Differentiating and Accommodating

From the information the teacher gained as students worked collaboratively, he or she is now able to offer instruction that provides guided interventions to students with similar needs. As the teacher does so, the others can read texts similar to those listed as suggested books or can be engaged with the Tech It Out! activity. They can also continue having text-supported discussions about thoughts they noted on their Interview/Conversation with a Character.

Beginning Level

After a read-aloud (e.g., *Goldilocks and the Three Bears*), students work as a team to answer a predetermined question asked by the teacher. Each student says one word, with the next student continuing with one word to answer the question and complete the sentence. This continues until the sentence is complete and the question has been answered. There are no wrong answers. Suggestion: After explaining the strategy, use five or six students to model the activity.

Question: *Goldilocks, which chair did you like best?*				
Student	1	2	3	4	5
	"I"	"liked"	"the"	"baby's"	"chair."

Intermediate Level

The activity for the intermediate level uses the same format as that for the beginning level task, but the teacher and students create a game show setting with a host (a student) asking the questions. The class becomes the audience and generates questions (oral or written) about the characters in a book. Questions are asked to a panel of three or four students, with each student answering in order, one at a time, until the answer is complete. There are no wrong answers; however, teachers should encourage students to answer more completely rather than with "yes" or "no." Using microphones from a technology station can add to the fun.

Question: *What would you do if Goldilocks had broken your favorite chair?*

Student	1	2	3	4	5	6
	"I"	"would"	"make"	"her"	"build"	"another" …

Advanced Level

Using the Question, Answer, Relationship (QAR) strategy (Raphael, 1986), students write questions about a text read aloud or independently. Students work in pairs as they write in-the-book questions (Right There, Think, and Search). Next, students write in-my-head questions (Author and Me, On My Own). When all questions are written, each pair of students switch questions with another pair. Answers are written and discussed. For more information on the QAR strategy, the teacher can check out the many sites that is typed into a browser.

Tech It Out!

Using a software program such as iComic or Comic Life and a digital camera, the teacher invites students to create comic book pages or graphic novels reflecting or extending the text being read. Their additions should indicate their understanding of the characters' perspectives. On the computer desktop, the teacher creates a folder of images that students may use that relate to or reflect the text, then asks students to retell the story in the comic bubbles. Printing out these pages, binding them, and putting them in a classroom library is a great way to motivate students as they read their own work in a creative form. To learn more about Comic Life in the classroom, the teacher can check out *www.eusd4kids.org/edtech/xapps/xapps_comic.html* or *plasq.com/comiclife*.

Suggested Websites and Books

www.teachersnetwork.org/teachnet/esl
www.alliance.writing (Teaching Diverse Learners)
www.teach-nology.com

DeSpain, Pleasant—*The Emerald Lizard: Fifteen Latin American Tales to Tell* (2005); August House.
Levitin, Sonia—*Silver Days* (1992); Aladdin.
Schlissel, Lillian—*Women's Diaries of the Westward Journey* (2004); Schocken.
Stanford, Natalie—*The Bravest Dog Ever: The True Story of Balto* (1989); Random House.
Taback, Simms—*Simms Taback's City Animals* (2009); Blue Apple Books.

References

Justice, L. M., & Sofka, A. E. (2010). *Engaging children with print: Building early literacy skills through quality read-alouds.* New York: Guilford Press.

McLaughlin, M. (2010). *Guided comprehension in the primary grades* (2nd ed.). Newark, DE: International Reading Association.

Melin, C. (2010). Between the lines: When culture, language and poetry meet in the classroom. *Language Teaching, 43*(3), 349–365.

Interview/Conversation with a Character

Conversation with _____

(Character)

Book Title: _____

Author: _____

1. What is the most important task you have accomplished? _____

   _____

   Why do you consider this accomplishment the most important? _____

   _____

2. In your opinion, what was the biggest problem you encountered, and how did you solve it? _____

3. What would you like to say to another character in this story or event? _____

   _____

4. What was the greatest personal motivation in your life? _____

   _____

5. If you could change one thing about your life or the outcome of the story, or an event, what would it be? _____

6. What did you enjoy most during the events of this story? _____

   _____

7. Who was the greatest support to you? Why? How? _____

   _____

8. What behavior of another character surprised, disappointed, or pleased you? Why? ____

   _____

9. What was an obstacle you encountered, and how can you learn from your experience?

   _____

10. What advice would you now give to use? _____

    _____

Personal Questions

1. _____

   _____

2. _____

   _____

3. _____

   _____

4. _____

   _____

5. _____

   _____

Composing with Computers

Common Core Standard

Introduce a topic clearly, previewing what is to follow; organize ideas, concepts, and information into broader categories as appropriate to achieve purpose; include formatting (e.g., headings), graphics (e.g., charts, tables), and multimedia when useful to aid comprehension.

TESOL Standard

Produce essays, poems, or brochures that address or pose creative solutions to multicultural issues.

Focus skill: Fluency
Secondary skill: Comprehension

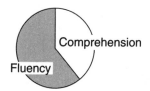

What Is the Purpose?

Use the Internet to research a topic, which is then shared.

What Is the Research Base?

Research documents the benefits of using computers to provide collaborative, interactive learning environments for second-language students. Web 2.0 contains an immense library of interactive authentic materials for the language learning classroom that can be used to enhance listening, speaking, reading, and writing skills (Cox, Jordan, Ortmeier-Hooper, & Schwartz, 2010; Jacobson & Lapp, 2010; Savage et al., 2010). *Composing With Computers* provides students with a template for developing a formal essay. Students can use information selected from various sources to develop an expository essay and present the finished product to class-mates.

Teacher Modeling and Guiding

1 After reading from a textbook or picture book about a content area of study, the teacher tells students that sometimes further research about a topic is necessary.

2 Using a projector or document camera, the teacher hooks up his or her computer to a screen for all to see.

3 The teacher models for students how to research a topic using Work Page 25.1, Composing with Computers. For example, while studying César Chávez the teacher may say, "As I think about what I just read from this book I still would like to know more about the life of Chávez. The book I just read doesn't give me enough details so I will search further about César Chávez, using a computer."

4 The teacher models for students how to search for additional text, images, and videos clips about a given topic.

5 The teacher introduces Work Page 25.2 and models for students how to take important facts from the Internet, then use the facts to construct main ideas and topic sentences (see Example 25.1).

6 After modeling a few important facts, turning them into main ideas/topic sentences, the teacher invites students to add to the model lesson. By doing so, he or she can check for understanding and guide students with prompts if needed.

7 The teacher models for students how to take the information on Work Page 25.2 and put it into a concluding paragraph on Work Page 25.3. These Work Pages should be copied back-to-back for students.

Peer Collaboration and Extension

1 During this time, students work in heterogeneous groups.

2 Students choose a topic (or are assigned one) for further research.

3 Students divide roles within the group. Two students can search for facts; one searches for images, and another searches for video clips.

4 Student groups compile information, using Work Page 25.2.

Important Facts

Topic: César Chávez

1. César Chávez's family moved from town to town in order to find work.
2. If the workers complained, the growers would fire them.
3. _____
4. _____
5. _____
6. _____
7. _____

Main Ideas/Topic Sentences

1. César Chávez provided service to others and dedicated his life to bringing justice, dignity, and respect to farm workers and to poor people.
2. _____
   _____
3. _____
   _____
4. _____
   _____
5. _____
   _____
6. _____
   _____
7. _____

EXAMPLE 25.1. Completed Work Page 25.2.

5 Once the information has been compiled, students work together to write a concluding paragraph about their topic.

6 The teacher saves time at the end of this lesson so that students can share their concluding paragraphs with the whole class.

7 As they work, the teacher moves among the students, offering cues and prompts and asking questions that support their performance. For example, for those who have collected many ideas but are struggling to write a summary statement the teacher might say, "You have a lot of facts here about your topic. Now identify which ones are most important. To do so, sort the main ideas from the details." For others attempting to write a conclusion, the teacher might say, "You have written your main ideas and topic sentences here. Now you can take a couple of these and think about how they might fit into a concluding paragraph."

8 The teacher also makes note of the similar needs existing among the students. This information can help him or her to offer later interventions to students with similar needs.

Teacher Differentiating and Accommodating

From the information the teacher gained as students worked collaboratively, he or she is now able to offer instruction that provides guided interventions to students with similar needs. As the teacher does so, the others can read texts similar to those listed as suggested books or can be engaged with the Tech It Out! activity. They can also continue having conversations supported by information they noted from their Internet searches.

Beginning Level

The teacher generates a list of "items" that need to be found on the Internet that are related to a theme, content topic of study, or literature/author study. Each student works with a partner to search for items requested. For example, during a science study on mammals, scavenger hunt items (questions) may include "Where do polar bears live?"; "What is the color of a polar bear's skin?"; "What do polar bears eat?" Students record answers and list the websites. After answers are found, students orally share their findings with the class. A discussion can be facilitated by the winning team (i.e., the pair of students who found the scavenger hunt items first).

Intermediate Level

A teacher-generated list of "items" can be written in a riddle form, using clues and key vocabulary from the area of study. Students search the Internet, recording answers to share with the class. Examples include: "What mammal, living at the North Pole, has transparent fur with skin the color of the night sky?"; "What mammal is a delightful dinner for a four-footed furry bear?"; "Name an animal found in the rain forest"; "Name two animals that are becoming extinct in the rain forest."

Advanced Level

During or after a unit of study (e.g., author study on Patricia Polacco) students think of their own items for their classmates to search on the Internet. Pairs or groups of students work together, talking about what to include on their scavenger hunt lists (e.g., What other books has Patricia Polacco written?). After orally drafting their lists and then writing them, pairs or groups of students can share lists with other pairs or groups. Each pair or group then creates an oral presentation for the class on the original topic they researched.

Tech It Out!

Students can experiment with font styles on a word processing program as they compose a newsletter, flier, obituary, letter, or biography about an author just studied. Using a scary font for an invitation is a great way for students to invite their spooky friends to a Halloween party. Students might use a FANCY font to write a summary of what happened to Cinderella and the Prince at the ball. The teacher makes sure to show lots of models of anchor texts to students before asking them to write. Word processing programs already come with many different fonts. For more font examples, the teacher may visit *www.shambles.net/pages/school/Fonts.*

Suggested Websites and Books

712educators.about.com/cs/technology/a/integratetech.htm
education.mit.edu/papers/GamesSimsSocNets_EdArcade.pdf
www.jamespaulgee.com/node/37

Ada, Alma Flor—*A Magical Encounter: Latino Children's Literature in the Classroom* (2002); Allyn & Bacon.
Delacre, Lulu—*Alicia Afterimage* (2008); Lee & Low Books.
Kovic, Ron—*Born on the Fourth of July* (2005); Akashic Books.
Lansing, Alfred—*Endurance: Shackleton's Incredible Voyage* (1999); Carroll & Graf.
Wilkin, Eloise—*Eloise Wilkin Stories* (2005); Golden Books.

References

Cox, M., Jordan, J., Ortmeier-Hooper, C., & Schwartz, G. (Eds.). (2010). *Reinventing identities in second language writing.* Urbana, IL: National Council of Teachers of English.

Jacobson, J., & Lapp, D. (2010). Modeling writing to enhance students' critical and creative thinking skills. *The California Reader, 43*(3), 32–47.

Savage, R., Erten, O., Abrami, P., Hipps, G., Comaskey, E., & van Lierop, D. (2010). ABRA-CADABRA in the hands of teachers: The effectiveness of a web-based literacy intervention in grade 1 language arts programs. *Computers and Education, 55*(2), 911–922.

Composing with Computers

Name: _____

A	B
Introduction: Paragraph 1	**Details About the Introduction**
_____ _____	_____ _____
Topic Sentence: Paragraph 2	**Three Details Supporting Paragraph 2:**
_____ _____	1. _____ 2. _____ 3. _____
Topic Sentence: Paragraph 3	**Three Details Supporting Paragraph 3:**
_____ _____	1. _____ 2. _____ 3. _____
Topic Sentence: Paragraph 4	**Three Details Supporting Paragraph 4:**
_____ _____	1. _____ 2. _____ 3. _____
Conclusion: Paragraph 5	**Details Supporting Paragraph 5:**
_____ _____	_____ _____

Information Sources:
Website/CD-ROM Titles:

1. _____

2. _____

3. _____

Important Facts and Main Ideas/Topic Sentences

Name: _____

Important Facts

Topic: _____

1. _____
2. _____
3. _____
4. _____
5. _____
6. _____
7. _____

Main Ideas/Topic Sentences

1. _____

   _____

2. _____

   _____

3. _____

   _____

4. _____

   _____

5. _____

   _____

6. _____

   _____

7. _____

   _____

Concluding Paragraph

Name: _____

Summarize the main ideas. Explain the importance of the topic. How is the topic relevant to people today? Is there a special connection to young people or to people in your local community?

_____

_____

_____

_____

_____

_____

_____

_____

_____

_____

_____

_____

_____

_____

_____

_____

_____

_____

_____

_____

_____

_____

_____

_____

_____

_____

Appendix

Charting Intervention Information

This resource guide is designed to help you chronicle the growth of each of your students in response to the interventions you provide. To use it, write the student's name in the first column. In the next column check the box identifying the focus of the needed intervention. The specific lesson or lesson segment that will serve as the selected intervention can be noted in column 3. After the intervention has been completed, and the student's performance reassessed, the final column can support your resulting reflections.

Student Name	Primary Intervention Needed	Details of Intervention	Response/Next Steps
	☐ Comprehension ☐ Pronunciation ☐ Fluency ☐ Vocabulary ☐ Writing		
	☐ Comprehension ☐ Pronunciation ☐ Fluency ☐ Vocabulary ☐ Writing		
	☐ Comprehension ☐ Pronunciation ☐ Fluency ☐ Vocabulary ☐ Writing		
	☐ Comprehension ☐ Pronunciation ☐ Fluency ☐ Vocabulary ☐ Writing		
	☐ Comprehension ☐ Pronunciation ☐ Fluency ☐ Vocabulary ☐ Writing		

Suggested Books Listed by Strategy Lesson

Explanation of the Language Fluency Levels

BEGINNING

The beginning level of language development includes speakers who are at the stages of preproduction, early production, and speech emergence. To accommodate their developing language, the books we have identified as **B–Beginning** include those that can be read aloud by a buddy or prerecorded so that students can listen while reading along. These selections have many pictures, visuals, few words (which are repetitiously presented), and a story structure that is predictable. This repetition of words supports the building of receptive vocabulary for preproduction speakers. Also included as beginning level books are those that support early speech production and emergence. Although still containing predictable text with many visuals, vocabulary is now contextualized in longer phrases and sentences.

INTERMEDIATE

Having approximately 6,000 active words in their vocabulary, students with an intermediate language fluency speak, write, and read more complex sentences and encounter more difficult concepts. Although still using visual supports, students are now able to grasp literature, science, and social studies content with the support of their teacher or buddies. Books identified as **I–Intermediate** offer supports to students as they infer, synthesize, and grow in understanding much of what they are hearing.

ADVANCED

Inasmuch as it takes between 4 and 10 years to be a fluent speaker of cognitive academic language in a second language, students having this degree of fluency function as do native speakers of the language. This is the stage at which English learners can exit supportive ESL programs, but support from classroom teachers should continue. Books that are identified as **A–Advanced** for reading by students with this language fluency are the same as those for their grade-level peers.

Strategy Lesson 1—Clues for Comprehension

B: Anonymous—*A Treasury of Mother Goose Rhymes* (1984); Simon & Schuster.
B: Lobel, Arnold—*On Market Street* (1989); Greenwillow Books.
I: Bunting, Eve—*So Far from the Sea* (2009), Sandpiper.
I: Soto, Gary—*Chato and the Party Animals* (2004), Puffin.
A: Lapsley, Arthur Brooks—*The Writings of Abraham Lincoln: Volume 2. 1843–1858* (2010); CreateSpace.

Strategy Lesson 2—Talking about Sounds and Words

B: Wright, Blanche Fisher—*Original Mother Goose* (1992); Running Press Kids.
I: Wyndham, Robert—*Chinese Mother Goose Rhymes* (1998); Putnam Juvenile.
I: Park, Linda Sue—*Bee-Bim Bop!* (2009); Sandpiper.
I: Torres, Leyla—*Liliana's Grandmothers* (2005); Houghton Mifflin.
A: Naylor, Phyllis Reynolds—*Shiloh* (2000); Atheneum.

Strategy Lesson 3—Sounding Out Words for Reading

B: Hamanaka, Sheila—*All the Colors of the Earth* (1999); HarperCollins.
I: Piper, Watty—*The Little Engine That Could* (1990); Grosset & Dunlap.
I: hooks, bell—*Homemade Love* (2002); Hyperion Books for Children.
I: English, Karen—*Nadia's Hands* (2009); Boyds Mills Press.
A: Hadaway, Nancy L.—*Breaking Boundaries with Global Literature: Celebrating Diversity in K–12 Classrooms* (2007); International Reading Association.

Strategy Lesson 4—Choral Reading

B: Hays, Anna Jane—*So Big!* (2003); Random House Books for Young Readers.
I: Perez, L. King—*First Day in Grapes* (2002); Lee & Low Books.
I: Grimes, Nikki—*Come Sunday* (1996); Eerdmans Books for Young Readers.
I: Schachner, Judy—*Skippyjon Jones in Mummy Trouble* (2008); Puffin.
A: Dahl, Roald—*Charlie and the Chocolate Factory* (2007); Puffin.

Strategy Lesson 5—Talking about Visuals

B: O'neill, Alexis—*The Recess Queen* (2002); Scholastic Press.
I: Williams, Karen Lynn—*Four Feet, Two Sandals* (2007); Eerdmans Books for Young Readers.
I: Sheth, Kashmira—*Monsoon Afternoon* (2008); Peachtree Publishers.
I: Woodson, Jacqueline—*The Other Side* (2001); Putnam Juvenile.
A: Baum, L. Frank—*The Wizard of Oz* (2008); Puffin.

Strategy Lesson 6—Role Play with Realia

B: Carle, Eric—*The Very Hungry Caterpillar* (2009); Philomel.
I: Lewin, Ted—*Horse Song: The Naadam of Mongolia* (2008); Lee & Low Books.
I: Ancona, George; Ada, Alma Flor; & Campoy, F. Isabel—*Mi Casa/My House* (2005); Children's Press.
I: Recorvits, Helen—*My Name Is Yoon* (2003); Farrar, Straus and Giroux.
A: Herlong, M. H.—*The Great Wide Sea* (2010); Puffin.

Strategy Lesson 7—My Reading and Speaking Log

B: Awdry, Rev. W.—*Thomas' ABC Book* (1998); Random House Books for Young Readers.
I: Katz, Karen—*My First Chinese New Year* (2004); Henry Holt.
I: Kurtz, Jane—*In the Small Small Night* (2005); Greenwillow Books.
A: Coy, John—*Around the World* (2005); Lee & Low Books.
A: Thomas, Joyce Carol—*Linda Brown, You Are Not Alone* (2003); Hyperion Books.

Strategy Lesson 8—Writing for Different Purposes

B: Hoffman, Mary—*The Color of Home* (2002); Dial.
I: Fox, Mem—*Whoever You Are* (2006); Sandpiper.
I: Mandelbaum, Pili—*You Be Me, I'll Be You* (1990); Kane/Miller Books.
I: McDonald, Megan—*My House Has Stars* (2001); Scholastic.
A: Bruchac, Joseph—*Our Stories Remember: American Indian History, Culture, and Values through Storytelling* (2003); Fulcrum Publishing.

Strategy Lesson 9—Total Physical Response with Pictures

B: Laden, Nina—*Peek-A-Who?* (2000); Chronicle Books.
I: Johnson, Angela—*Just Like Josh Gibson* (2007); Simon & Schuster Children's Publishing.
A: Li, Shuyuan; Chau, Aaron; & Wei, Deborah—*Walking on Solid Ground* (Aesop Accolades (Awards) (2004); Philadelphia Folklore Project.
A: San Souci, Robert D.—*Cut from the Same Cloth: American Women of Myth, Legend and Tall Tale* (2000); Putnam Juvenile.
A: Rockwell, Thomas—*How to Eat Fried Worms* (2006); Yearling.

Strategy Lesson 10—Expanding Word Knowledge

B: Boynton, Sandra—*Blue Hat, Green Hat* (1984); Little Simon.
I: Silverstein, Shel—*Where the Sidewalk Ends: Poems and Drawings* (1974).
A: O'Dell, Scott—*Island of the Blue Dolphins* (2010); Sandpiper.
A: Taylor, Mildred—*Roll of Thunder, Hear My Cry* (2004); Puffin.
A: Freedman, Russell—*Lincoln: A Photobiography* (1989); Sandpiper.

Strategy Lesson 11—My Read-Aloud Listening/Discussion Guide

B: Weeks, Sarah—*Splish, Splash!* (2000); HarperCollins.
I: Ada, Alma Flor—*I Love Saturdays y Domingos* (2004); Atheneum.
I: Steptoe, John—*Mufaro's Beautiful Daughters: An African Tale* (1993); HarperFestival.
A: MacLachlan, Patricia—*Sarah Plain and Tall* (2004); HarperCollins.
A: Twain, Mark—*The Adventures of Tom Sawyer* (2009); NewSouth.

Strategy Lesson 12—Word Maps

B: Iwamura, Kazuo—*Where Are You Going? To See My Friend!* (2003); Orchard.
I: Rawls, Wilson—*Where the Red Fern Grows* (1996); Yearling.
I: Esbensen, Barbara Juster—*The Night Rainbow* (2000); Scholastic.
A: Fleischman, Paul—*Seedfolks* (2004); HarperTrophy.
A: Hesse, Karen—*Out of the Dust* (2001); Klett.

Strategy Lesson 13—Scaffolding with Text-Supported Information

B: Seuss, Dr.—*The Foot Book: Dr. Seuss's Wacky Book of Opposites* (1996); Random House Books for Young Readers.
I: Stewart, Sarah—*The Journey* (2007); Live Oak Media.
I: Harrison, Troon—*Courage to Fly* (2006); Red Deer Press.
I: Wong, Janet—*This Next New Year* (2000); Frances Foster Books.
A: Crook, Connie Brummel—*The Hungry Year* (2001); Fitzhenry and Whiteside.

Strategy Lesson 14—Text-Supported Comprehension Guide

B: Wilhelm, Hans—*Hello Sun!* (2003); First Avenue Editions.
I: Levy, Janice—*The Spirit of Tio Fernando: A Day of the Dead Story* (1995); Albert Whitman & Company.
A: New Rider Weber, EdNah—*Rattlesnake Mesa* (2004); Lee & Low Books.
A: Edelman, Bernard (Ed.)—*Dear America: Letters Home from Vietnam* (2002); W. W. Norton & Company.
A: Anaya, Rudolfo—*Bless Me Ultima* (1999); Warner Books.

Strategy Lesson 15—Visualizing Steps in a Process

B: Karen Katz—*I Can Share: A Lift-the-Flap Book* (2004); Grosset & Dunlap.
I: Saenz, Benjamin Alire—*A Gift from Papa Diego* (1998); Cinco Puntos Press.
I: Gilchrist, Cherry—*A Calendar of Festivals* (2005); Barefoot Books.
I: Thien, Madeleine—*The Chinese Violin* (2001); Walrus Books.
A: Benjamin, Michelle—*Constellations: Twenty Years of Stellar Poetry From Polestar* (2003); Raincoast Books.

Strategy Lesson 16—Text-Supported Conversations

B: Sutherland, Margaret; & Lamut, Sonja—*Thanksgiving Is for Giving Thanks* (2000); Grosset & Dunlap.
I: Sekaquaptewa, Emory; & Pepper, Barbara—*Coyote & the Winnowing Birds: A Traditional Hopi Tale* (1994); Clear Light Books.
A: Jones, Ron—*The Acorn People* (1996); Laurel Leaf.
A: Eastman, Charles A.—*Indian Heroes and Great Chieftains* (2010); Nabu Press.
A: Dolan, Marlena—*Just Talking about Ourselves: Voices of Our Youth*, vol. 3 (1997); Theytus Books.

Strategy Lesson 17—Knowing How To Comprehend A Text

B: Rosa-Mendoza, Gladys—*When I Am/Cuando estoy* (2007); me+mi publishing.
I: Debon, Nicolas—*A Brave Soldier* (2002); Groundwood Books.
A: Wiesel Elie—*Night* (2006); Hill and Wang.
A: Duncan, Barbara—*Origin of the Milky Way* (2010); University of North Carolina Press.
A: Mahmoody, Betty—*Not without My Daughter* (1991); St. Martin's Paperbacks.

Strategy Lesson 18—Talking about Text: The Peer Tutoring Guide

B: Campbell, Rod—*Dear Zoo: A Lift-the-Flap Book* (2005); Little Simon.
I: Monk, Isabell—*Hope* (2004); First Avenue Editions.
A: Ravel, Edeet—*The Saver* (2010); Groundwood Books.
A: Ellis, Deborah—*Three Wishes: Palestinian and Israeli Children Speak* (2006); Groundwood Books.
A: Smith, Sherri—*Hot, Sour, Salty, Sweet* (2009); Laurel Leaf.

Strategy Lesson 19—Reading Comprehension Strategy Guide

B: Degen, Bruce—*Jamberry* (1985); HarperCollins.
I: Kimmel, Eric A.—*The Magic Dreidels; A Hanukkah Story* (1997); Holiday House.
A: Zlata, Filipovic—*Zlata's Diary: A Child's Life in Sarajevo* (2006); Penguin.
A: Bolden, Tonya—*Portraits of African-American Heroes* (2005); Puffin.
A: Palacios, Argentina—*Standing Tall: The Stories of Ten Hispanic Americans* (1994); Scholastic.

Strategy Lesson 20—Read, Record, Report

B: Rosen, Michael—*We're Going on a Bear Hunt* (2009); Margaret K. McElderry.
I: Choi, Yangsook—*The Name Jar* (2006); Dragonfly Books.
I: Nikola-Lisa, W.—*Bein' with You This Way* (1995); Lee & Low Books.
A: King, Laurie—*Hear My Voice: A Multicultural Anthology of Literature from the United States* (1993); Dale Seymour Publications.
A: Mazer, Anne—*America Street* (1993); Perfection Learning.

Strategy Lesson 21—Making Connections

B: Barton, Byron—*The Three Bears* (1991); HarperFestival.
I: Miller, J. Philip; & Greene, Sheppard M.—*We All Sing with the Same Voice* (2005); HarperCollins.
A: Alexie, Sherman—*The Absolutely True Diary of a Part-Time Indian* (2009); Little, Brown Books for Young Readers.
A: Stead, Rebecca—*When You Reach Me* (2009); Wendy Lamb Books.
A: Soto, Gary—*Buried Onions* (2006); Graphia.

Strategy Lesson 22—My Conversation Log

B: Taback, Simms—*Where Is My Friend?* (2006); Blue Apple Books.
I: Bunting, Eve—*A Day's Work* (1997); Sandpiper.
A: Applegate, Katherine—*Home of the Brave* (2008); Square Fish.
A: Blohm, Judith; & Lapinsky, Terri—*Kids Like Me* (2006); Intercultural Press.
A: Lowry, Lois—*Number the Stars* (1996); Laurel Leaf.

Strategy Lesson 23—Character Analysis

B: Lewis, Kevin—*Chugga-Chugga Choo-Choo* (1999); Hyperion Books.
I: Amery, Heather—*Stories from around the World* (2010); Usborne Books.
A: Crew, Linda—*Children of the River* (1991); Laurel Leaf.
A: McDonough, Yona Zeldis—*Who Was Harriet Tubman?* (2002); Grosset & Dunlap.
A: Staples, Suzanne Fisher—*Shabanu, Daughter of the Wind* (2003); Laurel Leaf.

Strategy Lesson 24—Interview/Conversation with a Character

B: Taback, Simms—*Simms Taback's City Animals* (2009); Blue Apple Books.
I: Stanford, Natalie Stanford—*The Bravest Dog Ever: The True Story of Balto* (1989); Random House.
A: Levitin, Sonia—*Silver Days* (1992); Aladdin.
A: DeSpain, Pleasant—*The Emerald Lizard: Fifteen Latin American Tales to Tell* (2005); August House.
A: Schlissel, Lillian—*Women's Diaries of the Westward Journey* (2004); Schocken.

Strategy Lesson 25—Composing with Computers

B: Wilkin, Eloise—*Eloise Wilkin Stories* (2005); Golden Books.
I: Ada, Alma Flor—*A Magical Encounter: Latino Children's Literature in the Classroom* (2002); Allyn & Bacon.
A: Lansing, Alfred—*Endurance: Shackleton's Incredible Voyage* (1999); Carroll & Graf.
A: Delacre, Lulu—*Alicia Afterimage* (2008); Lee & Low Books.
A: Kovic, Ron—*Born on the Fourth of July* (2005); Akashic Books.

Index